What does the Bible have to say to adults who suffer the debilitating emotional effects of growing up in an addictive, compulsive or hurting family environment?

Plenty, Melinda Fish explains in this recovery guide with a uniquely Christian viewpoint. **Adult Children and the Almighty** offers straightforward biblical advice to help adult children escape the emotional bonds of the past so that they can receive healing.

Melinda Fish addresses such important concerns as:

- What makes a hurting home dysfunctional?
- Facing the damage
- Restoring the wounded soul
- Taking the sting out of shame
- Overcoming a timid spirit
- Taking the pain out of memories

Through affirming counsel and clear Bible teaching, the author guides the reader to a new relationship with God. A relationship built on trust rather than doubt, hope instead of fear, and love that conquers anger and bitterness.

Melinda Fish writes, "Receiving emotional healing means taking the words you have heard, beginning to implement them and watching God restore your wounded soul to full health. You can choose to walk the pathway that leads out of the curse and into the blessing of the Lord. You can begin a new legacy now — for your days ahead and for your children and for their children.

"Do you wish to get well? Then may the Lord bless you as you move into His healing grace."

Adult Children and the Almighty

Melinda Fish

Published by
chosen books

FLEMING H. REVELL COMPANY
TARRYTOWN, NEW YORK

Scripture quotations are from the New American Standard Bible, copyright ©
The Lockman Foundation 1960, 1962, 1963, 1968, 1971, 1972, 1973, 1975,
1977.

Throughout this book where confidential experiences are related, fictitious
identifications are used, although the essentials of each story are true.

Library of Congress Cataloging-in-Publication Data

Fish, Melinda.
    Adult children and the Almighty / Melinda Fish.
      p.   cm.
    ISBN 0-8007-9178-9
      1. Adult children of dysfunctional families—Religious life.
    2. Christian life—1960–   I. Title.
    BV4596.A274F57 1991
    248.8′6—dc20   90-25777
                                               CIP

A Chosen book
Copyright © 1991 by Melinda Fish

Chosen Books Publishing Company, Ltd.
Published by
Fleming H. Revell Company
Tarrytown, New York
Printed in the United States of America

I lovingly dedicate this book to the glory of God, my heavenly Father, whose Fatherhood has been clearly shown me through the lives of four earthly fathers:

Dan Wilson, my father, whose courage, love and approval were always evident and who led me down the aisle the day I accepted Christ.

Vinton A. Fish, my father-in-law, who for more than twenty years has loved and accepted me as his own daughter.

Pastor A. J. Rowden, our father in the ministry, whose love and encouragement have inspired me to answer and fulfill God's call on my life.

William L. Fish, my loving, supporting husband and the father of my children, Sarah and Billy.

To these men I also dedicate this book.

I wish to express my heartfelt appreciation to the following people who helped make this book possible:

My mother, Merle Wilson.

My mother-in-law, Gladys Fish.

The many Christian "adult children" who shared their heartfelt experiences with me.

The members of the Church of the Risen Saviour, Trafford, Pennsylvania.

Len and Sandy LeSourd.

The members of the ACA recovery group, Episcopal Church of the Messiah, Virginia Beach, Virginia; George Stockhowe, rector.

My children, Sarah and Billy Fish.

Glenda Moser, Christian addiction counselor, Pittsburgh, Pennsylvania.

Chris Tabb, whose artwork appears in this book.

Ann McMath of Chosen Books, whose editing transformed the manuscript with sensitivity and expertise.

Jane Campbell of Chosen Books, who saw the vision for this book.

Contents

Adult Children and the Almighty

1
Starving for Love

Sherri had attended our church for only a few weeks when she made her first counseling appointment. I had watched as eager expectancy in her expression faded into anxiety. When she came in that Thursday morning—though I knew no details—I could guess that she was afraid her story would make me think she was unworthy to sit in the pew.

Sherri had grown up in the home of a closet alcoholic. This is a home where alcoholism is present but unrecognized and untreated. Her earliest scars resulted not only from her father's drinking but from early sexual molestation and from the trauma of watching her father carry on a twenty-year affair with another woman. As with his alcoholism, her mother had pretended the affair did not exist. Her brother had generally locked himself in his room as if to divorce himself from the pain, and Sherri had been the one her father turned to for "advice." He had confided in her many times about his unhappiness with her mother and his relationship with the woman at the office, and Sherri had given up feeling anything for many years, burying yet another secret in her private "closet."

Determining to leave the abusive atmosphere behind, Sherri had gone to college, but within the first semester had gone to bed with several men. One night at a fraternity party, several young men under the influence of alcohol had forced her into a bed-room, ripped off her clothes and gang-raped her. By then her sense of shame had driven her to her lowest level of despair and Sherri, unable to see how she could recover from this degrada-tion, held still another terrible secret for years. Her wounds festering, she had begun a ten-year string of relationships with men who abused her sexually and financially. During those years she had become pregnant by one man who married her, but the marriage ended in divorce only a year later when his physical abuse became too much for her to bear.

Sherri's life had made a turnaround when she and her mother attended an evangelistic crusade together and accepted Jesus Christ as Lord and Savior. For a few weeks things were different, but eventually, even though she attended church, she found herself gravitating toward men who abused her. It was the fact that she was currently involved in an affair that she felt powerless to cut off that brought her to my office.

Remorse seemed to fill her, and she cried tears of regret into tissue after tissue. Never had she found any release from the pain that strangled her soul and thwarted her Christian life.

"I feel sometimes as though I was born cursed . . . as though I never had a chance at a decent life," she sobbed. "I thought I could be different, but here I am—not much different from my father."

Sherri's story was not unlike many others that had been told me in the past fourteen years of pastoral counseling. I had long since stopped being shocked at the chaotic chronicles of abuse spilled out in my office. The details were always different, but my husband, Bill, with whom I co-pastor, and I had defined an emerging pattern, an order in the disorder of their lives. Although they lived in utter confusion, we saw common symptoms and behaviors. People like Sherri were victims, products of their own choices, true, but choices influenced by the sin-sick traditions of the homes they grew up in—traditions passed on from parent to child for many generations.

As Sherri and I talked, I remembered a conversation I had had with my sister five years before. Bill and I were living at the time in a large Victorian house in a declining inner-city neighborhood. Danna Kay had moved to the city and become involved in our church for a few months. Sitting at our kitchen table one day she asked me, "Melinda, have you noticed how it seems as if some of the people in our church—well, as if their mothers and fathers never taught them much of anything? You know, like how to act and what to do?" I had noticed all too frequently.

For ten years our church in the inner city of Pittsburgh had welcomed a parade of helpless, hopeless people. They sank into the pews, waiting there for help—single parents, addicts, the poor, the homeless and others who had suffered from growing up in troubled homes.

After each service the same ones always approached us looking for validation in a smile or advice about the simplest decisions of life in order to know how to behave appropriately. There were usually two or three in the children's ministry who could only be classified as "emotionally disturbed." Addicts were constantly among us, most of whom were still in denial—unable to face the extent of the wounds their compulsions left behind. And around them clustered a group of "crisis managers" who thrived on rescuing those untreated addicts from the results of their addictive behavior.

Now, for five years, our church has been located in the suburbs, and the problems we saw in the city are hiding here, too—

this time behind Estée Lauder perfume and Evan Picone suits. In both the city and the suburbs hollow and hungry eyes search our faces for something they hope Bill and I can give them.

Eyes like Sherri's. Other than the hurt there you would never have guessed her tale of woe. She was a professional career woman managing her own company, sophisticated and financially successful, but inwardly devastated. Had she come to me a dozen years before, I might have prayed with her, consoled her and sent her on her way hoping she would be O.K., and knowing she probably wouldn't. Now I knew that Sherri's problems could go away—but not without a process of healing that begins with the thing she and all others like her are missing: the ability to feel the unconditional love of God. This is but one of many healing aspects we will explore.

Adult Children

The majority of Christians sitting in pews today are victims of a curse, the influence of which began the day they were born. It's a curse dating to the Garden of Eden and it has touched their lives by tainting their childhood homes. As adults they are really children in adult bodies and will suffer the rest of their lives unless the curse is broken and its effects healed.

These children were brought up by parents who did not know how to love or teach about love. They were robbed of a crucial aspect of parenting by parents who were also robbed. These parents passed on a legacy of dysfunction—the inability to function properly—and begot another generation of divorce, poverty, abuse, alcoholism, addiction, compulsion and the unhealthy tendency to keep silent, hoping it would all go away.

When Bill and I discovered a few years ago that ninety percent of the adults in our church were themselves children of alcoholics and the remaining ten percent included victims of verbal, physical and sexual abuse, divorce and poverty, we began to understand that beyond preaching, we have, by entering the ministry in this last decade of the twentieth century, inherited another job: parenting adults who have been crippled by dysfunctional (nonfunctional) parenting.

And we are not alone. We have spoken on this subject in a cross-section of churches in a variety of states and have consistently found frighteningly high percentages in them as well.

But there are answers. This book is about adult children who, by the grace of God and the application of the healing balm of Jesus Christ, have left their legacies of dysfunction and broken the curse of wrath Paul speaks of in Ephesians 2:3. They have entered into the joy of becoming not children of wrath, but children of the Almighty. Instead of stumbling through life with hollow emotions and festering hurts, they are being renewed. They are learning to walk as children of God inheriting not a curse, but a blessing.

In the following chapters we will unfold the legacy inherited by the child of wrath. You will see how his or her unhappy home developed, the wounds it caused and his journey to healing—for himself, his children and those he influences in the world. You will read the stories of people like those around you who, though Christians, have struggled to keep their sanity and have overcome some of the most common painful experiences. At times, it will be unpleasant—maybe shocking and perhaps troubling to your heart. You will see those you love, maybe your own family or perhaps yourself, in their stories, but the answers in this book will help light the way to freedom.

Are adult children under a curse? What is a dysfunctional home? What makes it different from a healthy one and how can we tell if the homes in which we grew up were dysfunctional? Let's begin our journey.

2
The Family Curse

Are people like Sherri really under a curse? Are they doomed by a mysterious spell that alighted on their families as a result of the sins of their fathers? If so, why was Sherri's salvation experience, becoming a new creation in Christ, not enough to free her from such a curse? Are children supernaturally compelled to repeat the sins of their fathers or condemned to suffer the consequences of sins they did not commit?

These questions haunted me. If Sherri was cursed by the sins of her unbelieving father, why had prayer not lifted the burden? And if freedom could elude Sherri, what hope could anyone else have—for surely everyone's family tree hides a black sheep, a dark secret or an unconfessed sin somewhere in its foliage? I believe the answer for Sherri and for other children of dysfunctional homes lies in understanding what happened to Adam and Eve.

The Worst Thing that Ever Happened

I hope the bite of forbidden fruit was worth it! Scripture never tells us whether or not the man's and woman's taste buds tingled as the fruit's flesh filled their mouths. Adam and Eve probably never noticed the taste. Likely it was their first disappointment in life, the first in an endless chain of sorrows finally punctuated by their deaths—deaths that were never intended to happen. What we see now of God's creation is a mutation; it is all we have ever known. But the grief Adam and Eve experienced after the Fall probably has remained unequalled: They knew what it was like *before*.

The Bible says that after both the man and woman had tasted the forbidden fruit, they were emotionally affected immediately. For the first time they felt a rush of shame. They were startled into spiritual blindness. Their faces flushed with embarrassment over what had only moments before seemed so pure, and they felt uncovered, suddenly stripped before each other.

I believe that before the Fall Adam and Eve had literally glowed with God's glory—like Moses' face on Mt. Sinai. Now, knowing good and evil, they saw themselves as disobedient—sinful—and began to fear and abhor it. Bewildered they tried to relieve their sense of shame with an alternative. They tore into God's creation, ripping large leaves from a nearby fig bush and sewing them together, hoping to hide their shame. Perhaps they could postpone God's scrutiny with a bluff. It didn't work. The shame remained; and at the sound of the Lord God's approach, they cowered with fear.

We generally think about the disappointment and failure of the Fall from a human perspective, but I have often wondered how God felt when He called Adam and heard nothing but silence. To me, the saddest phrase in the Bible is, *Adam, where are you?* Adam was lost. Perhaps God felt the way a parent would to realize that his child is not where he left him. But His sorrow gave way to the searing pain of knowing His trusting friendship with His most prized creation had been betrayed. And Adam's and Eve's blame-shifting brought more disappointment. I don't think man ever knew how deeply He was loved by God or the emotional pain God suffered because of it. While God talked to Noah and walked with Enoch, not until centuries later, with Abraham, do we see God taking a human being as His friend.

When God's relationship with mankind was devalued and subordinated to a piece of fruit, He responded with righteous anger. The words live on and continue to produce an effect more devastating than any other words ever spoken. Through the curse God spoke, the creation, the serpent and the humans were all but finished. And because He could no longer trust Adam and Eve to stay away from the Tree whose fruit would make them live forever in their lost condition, He drove them out of the Garden and set at its eastern door angelic sentries and a flaming sword that flashed back and forth to guard the way to the Tree of Life.

The Curse

What was the ultimate reason for that prophetic pronouncement that contained such power we can never revoke it? Upon seeing that His creation had been contaminated by evil at the highest level, God cursed it so that one day it would come to an end. Rather than exist in sin-sickness eternally, it would be destroyed. And out of its ashes would be preserved men and women, some to eternal life with God and others to eternal life with the other god whose fellowship they preferred over His. In place of a now-flawed creation, new heavens and a new earth would stand in a perfect relationship with God forever.

The curse then was a manifestation not merely of God's judgment but of God's mercy, calculated to destroy, to invoke calamity upon the earth, the physical body and the soul in order to destroy Satan. Its existence presupposes the fact that eternal life exists and is far better than what we know of life presently. The curse also indicated that mankind would one day achieve victory over Satan and that redemption would come by a second Man, born of woman.

The Adamic curse contains several elements that have bearing on our lives, but because of the death and resurrection of Jesus Christ, they have limitations in the life of the Christian. The most painful element is that of separation from God and from others. The unity of fellowship that man and woman had with God and with each other before the Fall was much more intimate and fulfilling. And we never read again of their seeing God face to face or talking with Him in the cool of the day. Instead is the tone of loneliness and isolation, of preoccupation with survival.

Not only was man separated from God and others in a way he had never experienced, but he had lost his *authority*, the position and abilities that could only be characterized as supernatural in that they enabled him to care for a garden of the magnitude of Eden. For the rest of his life he would be at the mercy of creation rather than manager of it. He faced the humiliation of toil for that which only moments before had been so casually gotten. The sweat of his brow would be a constant reminder that life could have been much easier. And a "pecking order" would be established whereby he would have to rule his wife since he had not protected her from the wiles of the devil.

Added to that would be the pain of seeing the creation suffer because of him. The withering and dying of his surroundings would serve as a warning that one day he would also shrivel with age and return to dust.

What happened to Adam and Eve was terrible enough, but what happened to their children was worse.

The Curse Multiplied

Immediately after leaving Eden, Eve, so named because she was the mother of all the living, conceived and bore Cain who became a tiller of the ground. With the birth of a second son, Abel, the family of Adam and Eve seemed capable of functioning under the curse and making the best of it. But conflict arose between the two sons. Cain made an offering to God of the fruit of the field. Abel offered a more acceptable sacrifice by shedding the blood of a prized lamb.

When Cain realized that God not only preferred Abel's offering, but had no regard for his, he felt rejected and angry. His jealousy led to Abel's cruel murder.

Now God who had confronted his parents also spoke to Cain. "Where is Abel your brother? . . . What have you done? The voice of your brother's blood is crying to Me from the ground." And on Cain who would not admit his evil deed, God pronounced a curse that multiplied to him the pain and misery of the curse on Adam and Eve.

Biblical cursing doesn't stop there. Noah cursed one of his sons for seeing his nakedness while he was in a drunken stupor. Many of the patriarchs "prophesied" negative words over their children. Moses promised the children of Israel that curses would fall upon them in the new land if they ever turned from the God of Israel. Joshua echoed these warnings at the end of his life. The kings expected prophets to curse their adversaries before a battle. Indeed, cursing became a way of invoking calamity, taking vengeance and expressing disapproval. Those curses that were not directly from God usually proceeded from fear, anger and hurt. And those on whom curses fell took them seriously, fearing the doom they represented.

The Modern-Day Curse

The curse lives on as the world spins its way toward certain judgment. The exponential effects of Adam's curse have brought sorrow, pain, sweat, thorns and death in astronomical proportions. We have never had more knowledge or more pain and suffering. We have never had as many people or as much death. The earth has never been more in danger from human hands—pollution of oceans, air and streams, destruction of the land, extinction of species of animals, disintegration of the ozone layer. Whether people believe in God or not, they experience the effects of His words spoken ages ago.

These effects, which touch every individual in spirit, soul and body, are passed on from generation to generation through genetics. They are cultivated in physical surroundings and relationships. And they are passed on emotionally and spiritually by the actions of those whom we allow to influence us.

The principal incubator for the curse in the world has become the family. Originally designed by God to be a nurturing womb, the modern-day family has for the most part developed unhealthy traditions. It copes with the effects of Adam's curse by conforming to the ways of the world. The individuals who grow up in these dysfunctional families are often victims before they ever leave home. Instead of nurturing and tender care, they are exposed to some of the vilest acts of human nature.

In spite of the Church's emphasis on the family, the awful truth is being revealed that alcoholism and drug addiction have wrapped tentacles around nearly every family in America. In many of these homes, verbal, physical and sexual abuse have scarred the victims irreparably. And there are other "holisms" such as workaholism, the affliction of the baby boomer generation, a tradition learned from their parents, the survivors of the Great Depression. In these generations, in fact, a staggering 93 percent of American families no longer hold the traditional configuration of the father working and the mother staying at home with the children, according to a recent edition of *The Education Digest*. The rising divorce rate and the influx of women into the marketplace have brought the traditional family to the edge of extinction.

Families are functioning and shattering at an ever-increasing rate. According to a recent article in *Parents* magazine, the current divorce rate indicates that one-third of all children under eighteen years of age will experience the separation and divorce of their parents.

Other children suffer from dysfunctions of another type. They and their families live with the heartbreak of loved ones who are handicapped, chronically ill, disabled or mentally ill. In 1989 it was estimated that sixty percent of America's two million people with disabling mental illness lived with their families at least part of the time and hundreds of thousands more resided in nursing and boarding homes. This figure did not include the millions who are functionally psychotic and those who are undiagnosed whose strange behavior remains a mysterious source of shame.

Children brought up in these dysfunctional homes suffer debilitating emotional effects. Anxiety, depression and suicide are plaguing more and more children and young adults. To grow up with parents who were not there physically or emotionally or with parents who were not "normal" and able to assume their proper roles is nothing more than the curse of separation and isolation still at work. Still worse is the fact that the dysfunctional family has the uncanny ability to perpetuate its unhealthy patterns even when conscious resolve is made to do otherwise.

What About the Christian Family?

I wish I could tell you that there is a dramatic difference between the non-Christian family and the Christian family, that Christian families are by and large healthier and more functional. But fifteen years of pastoral counseling, speaking and praying with men and women in this country and abroad teach otherwise. The sin-sick traditions of a believer's family of origin continue to haunt him and repeat themselves in his present family years after he has come to Christ. These traditions, beliefs and roles and their resultant emotional problems bind the Christian and keep him from enjoying God, his life in the church and his Christian home as well as diminish his Christian testimony. For many people, being born again has brought a great sense of relief from the sins of the past, but it has failed to heal the wounds they suffered.

The Christian home is sometimes in greater peril because it is ashamed to admit that after several years of Christian growth it is still having problems. Often the problems exist but fester unnoticed for years because families—even those in the Church—are ignorant of the difference between a functional and dysfunctional home. It is often assumed that when parents and children come to Christ, all is new; the past, even the unresolved past, must quickly be forgotten. Some well-meaning teachers even argue that recalling the painful, unhealed events of childhood is undesirable, ungodly or unprofitable.

I used to be one of those people. I taught that once a person was saved and filled with the Holy Spirit, there was no need to deal with the past: You were now a new creation in Christ, all was forgiven, the slate was wiped clean and all problems could be resolved immediately and permanently through quick methods including more prayer, increased Bible reading and faithful church attendance. I did not know that a person's unresolved past can stifle his joy and smother his Christian life as much as the graveclothes would have smothered Lazarus if he had not been set free from them. There is available to us an added dimension of healing that can—and must—restore the soul and renew the mind if the believer is truly to break free of the curse of sin and death.

Breaking the Curse

Is a Christian really doomed to repeat the mistakes of his dysfunctional home? Does sin always repeat itself in successive generations? Will I die for my family's iniquity?

The truth is that even though the Adamic curse will be a constant source of hardship—we will not be freed from thorns and sweating toil in this lifetime—still, we can be free from the curse that grew out of it, the curse that touches our souls: This is the curse of the Law.

We must realize that the curse of the Law applies to individuals. In other words, no one need die because of the sins of his parents. Even in the Old Testament, God spoke through Moses, Ezekiel and Jeremiah that only when the tradition of idolatry was passed on and practiced by the next generation would they suffer the punishment for the iniquities of their fathers.

God spoke this through Ezekiel:

> "What do you mean by using this proverb . . . , 'The fathers eat the sour grapes, but the children's teeth are set on edge'? As I live," declares the Lord God, "you are surely not going to use this proverb in Israel any more. Behold, all

souls are Mine; the soul of the father as well as the soul of the son is Mine. The soul who sins will die. But if a man is righteous, and practices justice and righteousness . . . if he walks in My statutes and My ordinances so as to deal faithfully—he is righteous and will surely live," declares the Lord God.   Ezekiel 18:1–5, 9

Regardless of the sins of his parents, each person will suffer punishment for his own behavior. Curses are pronounced in the Bible in every case because of deliberate acts of sin. The only way anyone in a new generation can suffer from that curse is if he repeats that behavior himself and does not repent. "Like a sparrow in its flitting, like a swallow in its flying, so a curse without cause does not alight" (Proverbs 26:2). The God who extends mercy toward those who love and keep His commandments (Exodus 20:6) has always been eager to mitigate the effects of the curse immediately for those who turn from the sins of their fathers.

If this promise was available even in Old Testament days, how much more so now! When Jesus Christ died on the cross, He redeemed us from the curse of the Law—specifically, the curses pronounced by Moses on the children of Israel for failure to follow the specific and intricate commands of obedience in worship, work, meal preparation, etc. Because of Jesus' blood, we have forgiveness of sins and receive imputed righteousness. This is not based on our ability to keep the commandments, but because we have received a new nature from God almighty. Apart from the Adamic curse, no other curse can alight upon the righteous person who repents of his sin and claims the cleansing power of Jesus' shed blood.

So what is Sherri's problem? Why has she repeated the sins of her father? The answer lies in the wounds of her soul. Although the eternal consequences of her sins have been remitted by trusting Jesus Christ, the source of her present conflict lies in repeating the wayward behavior of her father. The way of escape for Sherri—and all of us—is as Ezekiel spoke: ". . . A son who has observed all his father's sins which he committed, and observing does not do likewise . . . he will not die for his father's iniquity" (Ezekiel 18:14, 17).

What will release Sherri is what will release anyone affected emotionally by the dysfunctional lifestyles of parents—observing with understanding and not doing likewise. In chapter 3, we will explore the elements, the weaknesses and the patterns of our dysfunctional homes in order to gain understanding about ourselves and how God wants to replace those ways with His.

3

What Makes a Hurting Home Dysfunctional?

Before we take a look at the elements that define the dysfunctional home take a pencil and answer *yes* or *no* to the following questions:

_____ 1. Did (or do) any of your family members including grandparents or great-grandparents have problems with any of the following areas?

a. alcohol

b. drugs

c. workaholism (especially parents not home frequently or distracted during "prime time" family hours)

d. sexual immorality (such as affairs, pornography)

e. anorexia or bulimia

f. obesity

      g. gambling

      h. mental illness (including chronic depression)

      i. handicaps, chronic diseases or debilitating health problems that were visible or affected their ability to function normally or socialize with others outside the family

      j. physical, sexual or verbal abusiveness

_____ 2. Were (are) your parents divorced or separated?

_____ 3. Did (does) your father or mother argue frequently?

_____ 4. Were (are) you afraid your parents or other family members might become violent or abusive with you?

_____ 5. Were (are) you afraid your parents would leave each other or you?

_____ 6. Were you afraid of being or were you left alone frequently for short or long periods of time as a child?

_____ 7. Were (are) you afraid of the temper of another family member?

_____ 8. Does (did) an immediate family member often call you names, threaten or embarrass you? Or can you recall a few searing words that affected you deeply?

_____ 9. Were (are) you ignored by your family members?

_____ 10. Have you ever been sexually molested?

_____ 11. Did any adult confide in you, a child, about his/her marital problems?

_____ 12. Do you recall feeling ashamed of the physical condition or behavior of one of your parents or siblings?

_____ 13. Were you ashamed of the house you lived in?

_____ 14. Did (do) your family members avoid recognizing or talking openly about certain subjects like a family member's drug or alcohol problem, handicap or disease, or subjects like finances that may have caused embarrassment, hurt or anger?

_____ 15. Was (is) your family socially independent, usually avoiding close contact with anyone outside the family and/or attempting to handle all difficulties without asking anyone for help?

_____ 16. Did (do) you feel emotionally manipulated by guilt projection, the "silent treatment" or intimidation and threats by a family member? (This does not include godly parental authority to discipline in a fair way.)

_____ 17. Do your parents place expectations on you as an adult that make you feel torn between them and your responsibilities to your current family or to your own goals for life?

_____ 18. Were (are) you often told how good your family was (is)?

_____ 19. Do you have problems such as communication difficulties with your spouse, family or other relationships, that are similar to those you had as a child?

_____ 20. Are you afraid of leaving home for fear the situation will deteriorate and the family members will suffer?

_____ 21. Did (do) you or any of your family members seem to feel that your accomplishments would raise the family's level of esteem in the eyes of others?

_____ 22. Did (do) you or any of your family members often feel compelled to rescue people from the consequences of their situations?

_____ 23. Did (do) you or any of your family members act like a diplomat, resolving conflicts between family members?

_____ 24. Did (does) one of your family members suffer as a victim of the irresponsible behavior or dysfunctions of another in the family?

_____ 25. Did (would) you feel relieved to escape your family situation through marriage, divorce or relocation?

Score: If you answered *yes* to as few as *one* of these questions, your family was/is dysfunctional to some degree. As you read on and observe the patterns and traditions of the hurting home, let God open your eyes.

The Home: Womb or Tomb?

Tonight when parents' cars pull up in driveways and the last children come in from a day's play, the front doors of homes all over the world will close. Some will close on scenes of happiness, but most will close on private dens of pain. For some the pain is too deep to be recognized because to notice and feel it would mean admitting a harsh reality over which they have no control. The day's activities have provided a brief respite, a distraction from what must now, as dusk approaches, be faced once again.

The word *dysfunctional* is too clinical to describe the scenarios that will unfold and the pain, sometimes physical but more often emotional, that will ensue from situations that never seem to change. *Dysfunctional* means not functioning according to a perceived standard of normalcy. And because the victims know no other way to live, they continue in a coping pattern not knowing there is a better way. Some who do know there is a better way still remain powerless to change their situations and escape the hurting environment.

The home as God planned it was to be a nurturing womb, a cozy retreat where each individual would be cradled in a protective sac. Cushioned by his parents from the harsh blows of life, he would emerge one day ready to enjoy creation, to enjoy his family and to know and enjoy God. In the womb he could be formed in clean surroundings hearing only tender voices, drinking in life, passing privately through awkward stages when to others he might be downright ugly. And one day he would move into a new dimension, mature enough to touch and be touched by others who had had the same delightful experience. His children, similarly formed and nurtured, would spread out and fill God's world.

The Elements of the Dysfunctional Home

But what happens to the child from a dysfunctional home is another story. The dysfunctional home has sustained a death blow to its vital organs, its members. It no longer provides an environment essential to the development of a Christlike, emotionally healthy offspring. Instead, the dysfunctional home hides a secret, forcing its members to limp along, falling short of its reason for being—to provide nurturing. Long before a child enters a family an "irritant" has been introduced: A stagnant, life-controlling problem becomes incarnate in a family member.

It may be the scourge of drug or alcohol addiction, the secret shame of sexual abuse or incest, the terror of physical and verbal abuse, or the more benign-looking forms of emotional abandonment found in workaholic parents—even those in the ministry. Beyond these addictive-compulsive behaviors are other problems that create dysfunction: chronic disease, mental illness, the death of immediate family members and the heartbreak over handicapped loved ones. These, too, make the growing child feel different or outcast and ashamed of feeling ashamed. Varied circumstances such as poverty or extreme affluence often cause the same reaction in family members as alcoholism.

1) The Problem Person

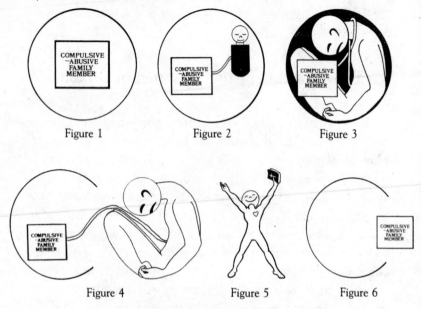

Figure 1   Figure 2   Figure 3

Figure 4   Figure 5   Figure 6

In this series of drawings we see how the dysfunctional home is invaded by what we will call a problem person. (See Figure 1.) The problem, represented by the square, remains rigid and unchanging, and all other persons conform to make it fit. There are two types of problem persons. One is the abusive person whose choices and compulsive behavior dominate the atmosphere. The other is a victimized person, one who was born handicapped or "different" or victimized by circumstances totally beyond his ability to change. The environment of the home is shaped by the presence of dysfunctional traditions, which we will examine later in this chapter.

Because of the presence of a problem person, the family suffers a sometimes mortal wound. Divorce may sever the home, dismembering the family into sore fragments. In homes where the parents do not divorce or separate, emotional wounds often continue to gape. Since the problem person's own needs are not met he is often—without intending to be—self-centered and preoccupied. A child is left to nurture and fend for himself. Because the child has no basis for comparing his home with that of his playmates, he sees his experience, at least in the beginning, as normal. But as he develops and comes into contact with other children from healthier situations or with those who mask their pain, the child of a dysfunctional home begins to see his home in a different light. (See Figure 2.) He may not be consciously ashamed of his circumstances, but he will begin to form a subconscious strategy for coping with his heartache, which may be felt only in fleeting, quickly quenched moments of private reflection.

Unlike the womb, which sets secure limits for a developing life, the dysfunctional home becomes a tomb, a facade of health covering the death on the inside.

2) The Victims: Enablers or Codependents

Around this problem develop the lives of the other family members who without realizing it become modified in their behavior and feelings to appease the problem person. This is known as being codependent. They are attached to the problem person by an invisible "umbilical cord" through which pass the problem person's attitudes and traditions. This unseen cord binds the members of the dysfunctional family passing through it not only some positive elements of camaraderie and love but also the dysfunctional traditions, roles and customs. This cord, like its natural counterpart, has the capacity both to nourish and to strangle, to be a channel for life or the instrument of death. Because the codependents are developing and not yet hardened in their ways, their initial flexibility causes them to mold themselves around the problem person who remains unchanged. The confining walls of the dysfunctional home and the rigid problem within serve as the parameters for development. (See Figure 3. We will return to these figures later.)

Distractions may move the problem into the background momentarily—the alcoholic may have sober periods, the fighting between abusive parents calms down or a relative comes to visit and the pressure is relieved. But the problem never goes away completely. Because it doesn't, the family members begin to adopt a coping strategy. During these cooling-off periods, dysfunctional families "harden" like wax into a common but abnormal pattern. This pattern includes the acceptance of certain beliefs, the unseen presence of traditional "do's" and "don't's," and the adoption of clearly delineated roles. Increasing evidence demonstrates that the degree of the presence of these patterns depends on the degree of the family member's exposure to the problem.

The presence of these patterns is modified only slightly by whether or not some of the family members are Christians. My years of counseling experience have proved to me that unless these patterns are consciously observed and corrected, they will continue and multiply, causing problems in the victims' spiritual lives and in their fellowship with other Christians, not to mention their marriages and children.

The Power of Tradition

The ability of the family to influence the outcome of its members is no more clearly seen than in the lives of auto racing's dynasties. If your name is Vukovich, Andretti, Unser or Bettenhausen, then each Memorial Day weekend—in fact, each May—is likely planned for the rest of your life. Regardless of where you live, you, your family and your racing team will migrate and set up camp at "The Brickyard," the nickname for the two-and-a-half-mile oval Indianapolis Motor Speedway.

Until I saw a glimpse of "Indy" myself, I never understood this tradition. Why would sons who have seen their fathers and uncles die on the oval launch their own racing careers and devote their lives to the pursuit of victory at Indy? Until I sat in the stands and felt the ground shake and the pressure of the air as the Indy cars howled and screamed by, I never understood the soul-tingling rush that draws not only the drivers but 400,000 fans to the largest single-day sporting event in the world.

I was fascinated by an article about the tradition of racing in the May 25, 1990, Greensburg, Pennsylvania, *Tribune-Review*. It described how Billy Vukovich, Jr., was listening to the Indy 500's 1955 race straining to keep up with his father's place when on the fifty-sixth lap his dad crashed into a lapped car and was killed at age 36. Thirteen years later Billy himself raced at Indy. Now his son races as well.

Tony Bettenhausen's father was testing a car for another driver when the car's front end fell off. The crash killed him instantly. Within months of his father's death, Merle and Gary had launched their own racing careers and Tony followed ten years later.

Mario Andretti's sons, Michael and Jeff, and his nephew, John, have all followed in his racing heritage. But why?

Tony Bettenhausen explained. "Why am I here? Because of the place and who we are. We're Bettenhausens. We're locked to Indy. But if I had a son, would I want him to come here to race? I'd like to think not. But the truth is, he'd probably be here because he is a Bettenhausen and this is Indy."

Tradition is so powerful that it can propel in spite of fear. It has a binding power that can survive all attempts to break it, including the admonition of what most mothers would call "common sense" and the invasion of outside influences like the opinions of others. People will often put tradition ahead of even God. That human beings are creatures of habit is so widely accepted, it is a cliché.

Tradition is established through a system of beliefs that result in behavior. These beliefs are not always rational or scriptural, but are more often accepted on the emotional level, and the dysfunctional family traditions are no different. Let's examine the following traditions of the dysfunctional family and their roots in the curse of Adam.

The Traditions of the Dysfunctional Home

1) The Tradition of Independence

Normal families interact socially with other individuals, families and groups in the community, but the dysfunctional family usually winds up isolating itself from others. Sometimes this isolation is involuntary, as when something abnormal about a family member or the family's condition of life causes others to feel uncomfortable around them. Perceiving rejection by society and feeling a sense of shame, the family members cling together sometimes in an unhealthy way. One common myth that encourages independence is the belief that "it's them against us."

This myth arises out of the sinful nature as a direct result of the curse of Adam. The feeling that the family is alone in its struggle comes from the isolation that everyone feels when separated emotionally and spiritually as well as physically from the God who created him (or her). Because he feels unprotected, he feels he must protect himself. Sometimes the bitterness of being rejected or perceiving rejection when it does not exist, almost anticipating it, causes the "it's-them-against-us" myth to become a self-fulfilling prophecy. When help is needed, the dysfunctional family is usually too afraid or too proud to ask for it. The belief that no one outside the family can be trusted to do what is right keeps the family further separated from others.

When an individual becomes a Christian, the tradition of independence can cause him to have difficulty developing healthy relationships. He will likely find it hard to humble himself to receive from others. He will also have problems with authority figures whom he may feel are out to take advantage of him. If he is thrust into authority himself, he will feel threatened and become more and more isolated. The person from a dysfunctional home must learn eventually that as a Christian, he has been placed in the Body of Christ to touch and be touched by others. In order to mature into Christlikeness, the tradition of independence needs to be broken.

2) The Tradition of Addictions and Compulsions

Increasing scientific evidence supports the claim that alcoholism is directly attributable to a genetic link in a large portion of alcoholics. Recent studies conducted by the University of Pittsburgh revealed differences in brain waves and brain chemistry between alcoholics and nonalcoholics. Still, exposure to alcohol and other addictive substances as a coping device in times of stress is the trigger to the development of addictions. The use of mood-altering substances and even processes like gambling or shopping splurges is a family tradition that can be handed down from generation to generation. Families who discover addictions among them can usually look back to their family trees to find this well-established tradition.

The use of mood-alterers and the development of addictions and compulsions have their roots in hidden anger and other emotional problems. These stem from turning to something other than God to fill emotional needs, as Adam and Eve did at the serpent's bidding in the Garden of Eden. When members of dysfunctional families become Christians, they are sometimes able to become freed immediately from the desire to use an addictive substance or process. As time goes by, however, cravings that have emotional and physical roots return. Unless the compulsive-addictive person knows the extent of his addiction and the keys to breaking its stronghold, the chain of this tradition will remain.

3) The Tradition of Abuse

Gus is a 38-year-old engineer and a victim of his father's verbal and physical abuse. When Gus was still in college, before he became a Christian, the fear of becoming abusive like his father and grandfather began to haunt him. One day he approached his psychology professor hoping to hear a word of encouragement that his fear was in vain. To Gus' dismay, his professor replied, "There's nothing you can do. You will become just like them." Not knowing that there is a divine solution to traditional abuse, Gus' professor knew only that children who are abused are more likely to become abusers than those who have never been exposed to this behavior.

Whether he or she strikes out with physical abuse that injures or kills, sexual abuse that robs a child of innocence and dignity, or emotional abuse that destroys a child's self-image, the abuser's inability to deal appropriately with anger is at the root of his or her behavior. The destructive nature of abuse comes to us from the Fall, seen in the degeneracy of Cain who killed his brother out of jealousy. Women who learn from their mothers that a wife's role includes surviving abuse often marry abusive men and find themselves living the same nightmare. The pain and suffering of the Adamic curse find their full vent on these helpless and innocent victims.

4) The Tradition of Silence

Underneath the tradition of silence is the deep-seated desire to maintain "peace at any price." The fear of having the dysfunctions discovered or discussed causes the family to be silent about them so that any further hurt or embarrassment may be averted. Anyone who violates this rule and begins to speak openly about the dysfunctions or the secrets of the family is perceived as a betrayer. Children who have suffered abuse are often warned that they will be punished if they tell anyone. They may be threatened with further physical violence or even death.

When Bill and I taught a course in a local Bible college on the family, we assigned the students to write a paper about the family in which they grew up. One part of the outline asked them to recall any hurtful experiences that they felt affected them presently. Several of the students who were still bound by the tradition of silence would not complete this part of the assignment, maintaining that the Bible exhorts us to think only on those things that are "of a good report." That same verse, however, talks about reflecting on things that are honest. I have found over and over that the most powerful messages a preacher preaches proceed out of lessons learned about the love of God from personal pain and suffering. The apostle Paul wrote, "Death works in us, but life in you." Until this tradition of silence is broken, the ministry of a person from a dysfunctional home will be hindered.

5) The Tradition of Denial

The inability to recognize or admit that problems exist—problems that make the family "different" or "ashamed"—is called denial. The tendency to deny what is wrong is a defensive tactic employed first by Adam and Eve when they realized they

41

had sinned, covered themselves with fig leaves and pretended nothing was wrong.

The root of denial is fear of a disclosure that will put them face to face with something they believe they cannot handle. Members of dysfunctional families will often deny completely the abuse or diseases they see present. In a survey of one hundred grandchildren of alcoholics conducted by Ann W. Smith in preparation for her book *Grandchildren of Alcoholics*, eighty percent reported that as children they were told repeatedly how "good" their families were. Straining to overcome the pain of their own pasts, their parents had misperceived the effects of the grandparents' drinking on their present families. In reality, the grandparents had passed on all the dysfunctional traditions we are studying in this chapter. In an effort to reach out for normalcy, the parents did not even tell their children for years that their grandparents were alcoholics. According to Smith, this denial led the grandchildren to feel that something was missing in their childhood development, but they were unable to determine the root. The fantasy that the family was "great," the members were "loyal," always there for you, was told repeatedly in an effort to reinforce denial about the family's true state.

The only way to find healing and break dysfunctional patterns is to come out of denial. Jesus Christ was always glad to touch and heal those who asked Him for help; He was hindered from helping those who would not come because of their unbelief. Today many Christians discourage persistent prayer or the confession of needs, disdaining it as a lack of faith. But real freedom comes when we are not ashamed or afraid to tell God, our family members or our Christian brothers and sisters anything that is true, when doing so is redemptive.

While I was attending a Christian writers conference, an elderly Southern lady, a real "magnolia blossom," joined us at the dinner table with her daughter. When I mentioned research information about families of alcoholics, she proceeded to extol the virtues of her husband, describing for fifteen minutes what a good husband and father he was. This dear woman, not realizing her comments were a defensive reaction, painted an almost saintly picture of Charles. Minimizing his faults, her own pain and that of her daughter, she said, "Of course, he had to have his 'nip' and couldn't give up the bottle. . . . He just never could seem to get rid of that nasty habit . . ." and continued magnifying his virtues. She didn't know that she purposely blotted out painful memories and recalled the past selectively, portraying it to others the way she had wanted it to be—not the way it really was. Her daughter stared at her plate, finishing her meal hurriedly, and looked relieved when the subject finally changed. This inability to perceive the whole picture is characteristic of families in denial about the presence of alcoholism and the degree of its effects on every loved one involved.

6) The Tradition of Rigidity

The presence of an unpredictable problem such as alcoholism or abuse in a family causes the other members to reach out for tangible absolutes, islands in the stormy sea of dysfunction. Children of dysfunctional families tend to cling to rules and expect them to be followed rigidly or else circumstances to remain the same. Underlying this behavior is the myth of permanence whereby the children of dysfunctional families fantasize about a stable, perfect home that never changes.

The tradition of rigidity causes grown-up children from dysfunctional homes often to decide impulsively on a course of action without giving enough consideration to alternatives. This tendency creates stubbornness and sets the adult child up for much disappointment and suffering in the long run, as does expecting the conditions of life always to be the same. Loved ones die, people change interests, relationships deteriorate and intensify and circumstances are altered by the uncontrollable decisions people make. In the middle of this, the adult child tends to find emotional adjustment difficult. When his source of permanence and stability fails to provide the needed security he overreacts, sometimes with compulsive acts of self-punishment or self-deprivation.

Adult children of dysfunctional homes tend to gravitate toward churches and organizations with rigid rules and expectations and tend to interpret the Bible to the letter of the law. To think that the will of God may sometimes be unpredictable is unnerving for them. They are far more comfortable in settings where the rules stay the same. In passing on the legacy to their children, they may say things like, "We Smiths do it this way."

Religious tradition, including denominational affiliation or lack of it, is handed down from generation to generation. It is interesting to note that during the recent charismatic renewal thousands of people violated the religious heritage of their parents and switched denominational affiliations. Every member of our local church, for example, comes from a denomination different from that of his or her parents. And great have been the unnecessary wounds of rejection and intimidation from their parents caused by choices they should have been free to make as adults.

7) Traditions of Dysfunctional Communication

Members of a dysfunctional family operating in the traditions of silence and denial usually communicate with each other indirectly. Tiptoeing on eggshells, being afraid to speak to the party in question about how he or she really feels, they employ manipulative methods to make things happen or to get their views across.

Triangling is one avoidance technique. It means using a third party to say things to another person that someone feels awkward saying for himself. One woman in her early twenties who was being put into the middle of her parents' fighting called me on the phone begging me to talk to her mother. Her father was verbally abusive and her mother, having lived with his rages for more than thirty years, was in the habit of using her children to give him the messages she was afraid to deliver. But now, initiating triangling on her own, the daughter wanted me to become the carrier pigeon.

The tactic of triangling when employed in the workplace can wedge a barrier between employees and the boss. In the church some leaders become the third angle of the triangle by delivering messages from the congregation to the pastor. My husband, the senior pastor of our congregation, refuses to hear messages through others, encouraging those who deliver them to stop this practice. We have noticed that those who send messages through others and those who deliver them are always adults who grew up in homes with major dysfunctions and are usually unnecessarily afraid of authority figures. This fear also manifests itself in an inability to confront or express important feelings or ideas—even positive ones—for fear of being rejected.

When Adam and Eve sinned, they dreaded facing God. When He confronted them, Adam tried to hide behind Eve, and Eve behind the serpent. People have been triangling ever since, but not always because they have sinned. Adults from dysfunctional homes who have a low sense of self-esteem and feel unsure of how they will be accepted fall easily into triangling. People who become carrier pigeons for messages usually wind up becoming garbage dumps for gossip because they have a listening ear. Adults and children who have played the role of placater in their dysfunctional homes seem exceptionally vulnerable to triangling, although it is a tradition that affects each member of the family.

Another avoidance technique in communication is *intimidation.* Also based on a low sense of self-esteem, intimidation is a tactic employed by more aggressive adults from dysfunctional homes. Intimidation is usually learned from the abusive problem person in the family and involves overt or veiled threats. Something will be withdrawn or imposed if his or her demands or expectations are not met. Intimidation plays upon the fear and uncertainty that is common to all family members in dysfunctional homes.

How many church leaders have been intimidated by adults who threaten to leave the church if the leaders do not conform to their expectations? How many parents threaten to abandon or deprive their children of affection and rewards if demands are not met? How many bosses threaten to fire employees when they never intend to do so?

Indirect manipulation is another kind of avoidance technique. Rather than speaking directly to others, it is easier to set the stage, to move chessmen into place in order to make your move. Who can forget Lucy's and Ethel's constant humorous manipulation of their husbands, Ricky and Fred, on the TV sitcom "I Love Lucy"? But most indirect manipulation is far from humorous and those who feel set up by it will grow to resent being manipulated.

Keeping secrets is another form of dysfunctional communication that proceeds directly from the tradition of silence. To protect one family member from the emotional impact of realities, others in the family are frequently told to keep secrets from each other and the outside world. This puts pressure on the secret-keeper. What will happen to me if the secret is somehow divulged? Will I be punished or scolded? Furthermore, the secret-holder must shoulder the emotional impact of the secret, being unable to share the burden. This promotes the traditions of silence and denial.

Keeping secrets prevents emotional maturity. It is almost always a means of control and manipulation whereby the secret-sharer tries to become the clearinghouse for information.

8) The Tradition of Martyrdom

The children of dysfunctional homes are survivors who have learned an array of coping skills to make it through the toughest situations. But survival breeds a victim mentality, a particularly specious belief that can permeate the thought life. The victim mentality, the idea that I was created to suffer, barely to get by, that my lot in life is to be subservient to others, often masquerades as real Christianity and is the core belief that develops into codependency.

Fixing situations and people, rescuing them from their troubles and striving to come up with the solution to others' problems, is a tradition handed down in every dysfunctional family. This can rightly be called an addiction—a "people addiction"—for it is as surely a mood-alterer as any other substance or process. The tradition of martyrdom implies that one's only reason for living can be defined in terms of another.

When Adam and Eve fell and became separated from God and His Garden, they felt out of context because they were. When a person cannot sense the unconditional love of God, he tries to compensate by finding meaning in terms of being beneficial to others. His usefulness validates him as a person. What he does, rather than who he is, gives meaning to his existence. The basis for this belief is not Christian. Jesus Christ did nothing from self-doubt or the inability to sense His Father's presence, but because He knew who He was and desired to obey His Father. True ministry proceeds out of confidence in God's personal love for you. God's love becomes the constraint rather than the emotional need for validation. It is sometimes hard to determine the motives behind our actions, but martyrdom for its own sake usually manifests itself in fruitless toil and emotional drain.

Adults from dysfunctional homes feel compelled to martyr themselves for causes and people. They are not motivated by genuine love for those in need. They may be seen en masse at anti-abortion demonstrations looking forward to stints in jail, carrying placards at pornography establishments, spearheading campaigns for the homeless, collecting funds for various diseases, ministering compulsively and otherwise driving themselves to find validation for their lives.

When our church was located in the inner city, the constant parade of needy people through the doors attracted many Christians from the suburbs and nearby universities who seemed to need involvement in pathetic situations to validate themselves. As long as the church was involved in pursuits they felt were noble, they remained supportive. When the building we met in was scheduled to be torn down, however, and the only place we could relocate was in the suburbs, their cause disappeared. They couldn't cope with not feeling needed by the needy. Many of them left the church unable to see and receive the Lord's blessing, reward and opportunity for growth in our new situation.

The power of tradition binds the individual to "cursed" ways of behavior. Traditions are usually emotional rather than rational, but in order to make them appear justified, the family enforces them as solid, divine principles.

This is only part of how the lives of the children of dysfunctional homes are thwarted. In the next chapter, we will explore the emotional damage that growing up in a dysfunctional home inflicts on its members and we will begin learning how Jesus Christ can restore the soul.

4
The Hurting Child

The traditions of the dysfunctional home and the presence of a "problem" like the ones we have mentioned cause untold grief to family members. The scars they bear can remain in their emotions for a lifetime, affecting their marriages, their relationships with others outside the family and their spiritual lives. But no scar is so deep that the healing power of Jesus Christ cannot touch it and heal it. The pathway to healing is rocky, however, and sometimes obscure, filled with shadows and pitfalls that can frighten the anxious child within. In order to find the healing touch of Christ, it is necessary to present the wounds to Him. Jamie Benson's path to healing began with a secret of which he was terribly ashamed. As you read his story, see how the traditions of his dysfunctional home affected him emotionally. As we begin to understand how the soul can be damaged, we will see why the mind must be renewed for healing to begin.

Jamie's Unhappy Secret

"I would rather my mother had had cancer than this!" cried Jamie Benson in the pastor's study. Jamie was 35 years old at the time of this confession, but the painful experience of growing up with a mother who was diagnosed officially as paranoid schizophrenic left scars that lingered long after his mother's funeral five years before.

Jamie's deep sense of self-doubt was directly attributable to being reared by a mother who read meaning into even the smallest details of life.

Jamie cannot remember how old he was when his mother first told him she was being monitored by a research group that was testing methods of psychological warfare on her. When the family's old Victorian house creaked in the wind, his mother explained to him and his sister that the sounds were attempts by the research group to harass her and keep her from sleep. Car license plates with certain letters and numbers were all part of the conspiracy to "break" her. If ambulances sounded their sirens during the night, she nodded knowingly in the morning.

Sometimes the pressure of her thoughts drove Jamie's mother to the brink of a nervous breakdown. During those times she stayed awake at night, pacing the floor, and Jamie came to dread the sound of his mother's steps above his room as much as an alcoholic's child dreads the sound of breaking glass or the guttural grunting of a drunken stupor.

His mother's paranoia was manifested in other ways as well. She was a meticulous yet frustrated perfectionist. She wore a frown and bore the gut-level belief that God demanded a strict standard of righteous living, which she was obligated to uphold. This drove her to expect unrealistic perfection from others. She corrected Jamie's and his sister's every move, analyzing and categorizing every opinion. She feared the downfall of the government and stored reserves of plastic cartons, old canned goods and mildewed clothes in the basement. "Mother wouldn't let us throw away anything. By the time she died, there was left only a small path through each room of the house."

Jamie rarely invited friends over. The family's few attempts at socializing had been disasters. On one occasion, his mother picked the minister's sermon to pieces as the minister sat at their table and then began to unveil her story about the research group's secret plot against her. At church, the family sometimes made excuses for his mother, but after a while, people stopped asking. Jamie's father, a picture of stalwart grace, never talked openly about his wife's mental illness. When he referred to it, he simply said in hushed tones, "You know how your mother is."

Jamie's feelings for his mother alternated between deep pity and hatred. His resentment of the situation deepened through his teenage years, and he often wished he could escape and go home from church with one of the other families who led happy lives. He envied them secretly but found himself criticizing them mercilessly as his mother would do.

Jamie's drive toward workaholism as an adult started in school. His superior intellect manifested itself early and he knew it would prove to be his ticket out of the malaise. Partly to ensure his escape and partly to save the family from total disgrace, Jamie drove himself to excel at school and won an engineering scholarship to a top university.

In his senior year Jamie met and married Stephanie, the only girl he had ever dated. She seemed to be the doting wife who would meet his every need, but three years into the marriage, communication problems brought them to a standstill. Jamie found himself frozen in his ability to demonstrate affection and often hid from her behind his work load. She nagged him constantly and he employed the tactic of passive resistance, which frustrated her more deeply. It was the troubled marriage that led Jamie to the pastor's office for counseling. The insights unfolded there put into his hand the key to freedom from the wounds left behind by his family's past.

King Saul's Dysfunctional Home

Believe it or not, dysfunctional homes like Jamie's are not without a biblical parallel. Jamie's home life was a startlingly close model of the tortured King Saul's situation. I would like to mention it here briefly because in the life of his son Jonathan we see tragic effects of a dysfunctional home. Unlike Jamie, Jonathan was unable to break the traditions that bound him.

For Saul's family everything seemed normal at first, but worsened almost overnight, plunging the family into a nightmare. King Saul was chosen against his will to be the first king of Israel. The Scriptures indicate that low self-esteem was compelling him to hide behind the baggage when the day of his ascendancy to the throne arrived. This most handsome of Israel's men was all but dragged before his waiting subjects.

But as power usually does, it finally wooed its victim into a state of complacency. At first, Saul's zeal against the Philistines seemed to be driven by God alone. He battled the enemy successfully and his fame grew.

Then several deliberate acts of disobedience to God turned the tide of his life and damaged his family permanently. It had been God's plan to use him and establish for Saul an enduring kingdom, but when Saul's compromising heart drove him to save the contraband spoils of battle for himself, the prophet Samuel placed a curse upon him, tearing the kingdom from him. The anointing of God departed, and what the Bible calls "an evil spirit from the Lord" (1 Samuel 16:14) tormented him with symptoms not unlike those of modern-day manic depressives.

Overnight, it seemed, King Saul, imposing at a height head and shoulders above any man in Israel, began to have sporadic fits. He raged like a madman through the rooms of his palace. The most tragic player in the whole story was Jonathan, King Saul's son, who, like Jamie, became a victim.

The traditions of the dysfunctional home—independence, denial, rigidity, abuse, silence, poor communication and martyr-dom—were all active in Jonathan's home.

The presence of these traditions in a family causes the members to take on certain roles. These roles have been almost universally adopted in some form by counselors to describe the pattern of behavior exhibited by those suffering from a source of shame. Usually each member, reacting to the violence or source of shame, confines himself to one major role, although some vacillate between roles. These include the *hero* who excels outside the family to prove the family's worth; the *placater* who shuttles diplomatically between family members, refereeing conflict and smoothing down feathers to prevent emotional outbursts; the *scapegoat* who either gets blamed for the problems in the family or creates new ones that rival those of the problem person in magnitude; the *mascot* who cheers the hurting family by joking and otherwise diverting attention from the problem; the *martyr* who is usually but not always the spouse of the problem person, suffering on his or her behalf; the *rescuer* who leads the family in saving the problem person from the consequences of his abuse; the *lost child* who fades into the background, escaping his pain silently by living in a fantasy world; the *victim* who sometimes receives the brunt of the problem person's anger; and the *abuser* who is not always a parent but can be a child on drugs, for example, whose problem or dysfunctional behavior is responsible for this drama.

Almost everyone in a dysfunctional family will fall into and maintain these roles. Psychologists Hemfelt, Minirth and Meier in *Love Is a Choice: Recovery for Codependent Relationships* make this observation:

> These roles help codependents survive their family and the members learn them well. But the roles are warped. Anomalous. When they are applied outside dysfunctional situations, as for instance in employment, church and friendships, they don't work. The rules have changed; the relationships differ, healthy people are involved now. And yet, the family members who came to depend upon the old rules don't know how else to play the game. The codependents are stuck with a twisted system of interpersonal relationships that cannot help them cope with the real world.

Through the development of these roles, which are really traditional ways of reacting to and masking pain, the curse or tradition is guaranteed to be passed on. Even when people accept Jesus Christ and receive the Holy Spirit within, the souls of these victims can remain warped in these molds or adopt new roles to fit the situations in their new Christian family and in all other interpersonal relationships. A conscious effort must be made to break tradition and let healing occur.

Jamie's family was no different. He could see the roles in himself and in his father, mother and sister. Jamie recognized himself as the hero, and as is common to other heroes, Jamie developed workaholism. Jonathan, the son of Saul, seemed to play several roles. He played the hero by initiating conflict with the Philistines and excelling in battle—"Someone has to obey God around here." He placated and refereed the squabble between his father and David. He became the scapegoat during his father's tirades of verbal abuse when Saul cursed him and blamed him for betraying the family, projecting onto Jonathan his own awareness of failure. He became a victim, dodging the spear his father hurled at him in a fit of rage, almost killing him. And he became a martyr, following his father into battle against the army of his best friend, when all along God had given him the supernatural grace to love and serve David, the one who would replace Saul as king. But he died in battle a victim of his dysfunctional home and the tradition perpetuated by the myth of "loyalty regardless."

I wonder if Jonathan's mortal wound was any more painful than the emotional wounds he suffered. It was probably not nearly as painful as the words of rejection and contempt and the pain he felt from his father's unpredictable rages. Like Jamie, Jonathan suffered silently, but unlike Jamie, who found help, Jonathan's wounds killed him. Jonathan could have lived, an effective tool in the hand of God enjoying the victories that God brought to David, but the wounds in his soul, as is true with everyone, affected his spirit. Instead of being led by the Holy Spirit, he was led by his wounded soul. This is the tragic pattern of the codependent. Let's look at this relationship.

The Dysfunctional Soul

The way the emotions affect the spiritual life will always remain a mystery to the Christian until he understands the relationship between his body, his soul and his spirit. According to the apostle Paul, man is not only body and soul, but also spirit, a tripartite being made in the image of God (1 Thessalonians 5:23). The word *soul* comes from the Greek word *psuche*, which means "mind." Within the mind reside thoughts, emotions and an independent will. Until a person comes to Jesus Christ, his spirit is dead as a result of sin. His soul and body have governed themselves only according to their own *sinful* will. But once he receives the indwelling Holy Spirit, his human spirit is alive, renewed with the life and strength of almighty God.

Now the soul and body, which are used to being in complete control of thoughts and actions, resist being deposed from their position of authority. The new believer wants to set aside his appetites and lusts and follow the new spirit inside. He wants to be led of the Holy Spirit, which is the evidence of our adoption into God's family.

Soon he learns, however, that this is not accomplished so easily. In fact, warfare breaks out between his mind, will, emotions and body and his newly regenerated spirit. Paul talks about this conflict in Galatians 5:16–17: "Walk by the Spirit, and you will not carry out the desire of the flesh. For the flesh sets its desire against the Spirit, and the Spirit against the flesh; for these are in opposition to one another, so that you may not do the things that you [the fleshly you] please."

Watchman Nee, in his Christian classic *The Release of the Spirit*, wrote,

> In His dealing with man, God's Spirit never by-passes man's spirit. Nor can our spirit by-pass the outer man (soul and body). This is a most important principle to grasp. As the Holy Spirit does not pass over man's spirit in His working in man, no more does our spirit ignore the outward man and function directly. In order to touch other lives, our spirit must pass through the outward man.

In other words, the soul is the organ of expression for the spirit. It should not rule the body, but it often does through our dysfunctional traditions, damaged emotions, contrary attitudes, addictions and compulsions.

I have noticed in many Christians an attempt to deny self, to put to death the soul and body, to swallow anger and frustration and deny the soul any life at all. A person can fall into religious addiction, actually denying the worth of emotions and claiming that the spirit can bypass the soul completely. The soul with its desires and emotions is rejected as wicked rather than seen as an organ that can be used by the Holy Spirit to love, to feel joy, to experience peace. This view is unhealthy to say the least. The soul will be joined with the spirit and body until the day we die. Its restoration to full use, therefore, is necessary to fulfill God's wonderful plan for our lives. This restoration takes place by the process known as the renewing of the mind.

The Renewing of the Mind

The dysfunctional home conforms the family members to traditions, roles, habits, attitudes and ways of thinking that are ungodly. But until an individual's mind is renewed by the Holy Spirit, who now resides within, the mind will be a prison for the spirit. Yet the fact that the Holy Spirit now lives inside does not automatically guarantee that the mind will be renewed.

Think of the soul as the desert in Israel that God promised would blossom. Today that desert blossoms and bears fruit even as the prophet spoke, but only as a result of irrigation, water springing up in its waste places. The Holy Spirit can spring up like a geyser, too, watering the barren soul of man, transforming the arid landscape into a lush orchard. This springing up of the Holy Spirit renews the mind with revelation—that is, He unveils to the human mind understanding from God's reservoir of wisdom. This revelation has the ability to enlighten the soul, to free the soul from thought patterns, habits and ways of the past and replace them with God's ways.

Paul commanded the church in Rome to allow this process to take place: "Do not be conformed to this world, but be transformed by the renewing of your mind" (Romans 12:2). It is within our power to release or quench the Holy Spirit's healing power. We can block the mouth of the well. Or, like Jamie, we can open up to Jesus Christ and let the Holy Spirit within restore the soul.

Jamie's Key to Healing

When Jamie came for counseling, he feared that his spiritual renewal had somehow been deficient. Once he began to understand that his problem was not in a deficient conversion experience, but in his dysfunctional soul, he opened up to God, to his pastor and to his wife. "All along, God wanted to love my wife through me, but I couldn't because of the wounds of my past."

Jamie had let his dysfunctional soul convince him to hide in the fig bushes of workaholism and to avoid communication. His spirit had been held captive by his unrenewed mind. He believed and acted in many dysfunctional ways that hindered the Lord's working through him. But through several years of counseling, trading old processes and patterns for more steps to freedom—steps we will be discussing throughout this book—and learning to allow the Holy Spirit to spring up within, Jamie is being restored.

In the past fifteen years of our ministry, Bill and I have met many people like Jamie. Whether or not they are healed depends on their depth of surrender to God's healing process. Healing begins with the understanding of the dysfunctional home, how it incubates the curse and wounds the soul and how the healing power of God's Spirit can renew the mind. Let's examine the next step in the process.

5
Coming Out of the Womb

Glenn is the elder son of an alcoholic father. His mother works as a waitress to help pay off debts. Sometimes while coming out of his alcohol binges, Glenn's father, George, regrets the financial strain his drinking places on the family. (He bought a truck on one occasion and charged up several thousand dollars on a credit card on another binge.) But instead of dealing with his alcoholism by entering treatment and attending a support group, he tries to soothe his aching conscience by "making it up to Lisa," his wife of 27 years.

Glenn has felt responsible to help from the time he was in elementary school. He finds jobs and gives most of his earnings to his parents, who have been on the edge of bankruptcy several times. And when his father has too much to drink in the bar down the street, Glenn is the one who retrieves him from his chair in the corner and supports his weight while he stumbles home. All the way home, his father leans against him and keeps saying how sorry he is that he drinks too much and promises never to do it again. But Glenn doesn't listen. He knows it's only a matter of a few days or weeks before he will have to help his father home again.

Glenn has the desire to pursue a career in law. His chance at law school has come in the form of a work study grant at a college two hundred miles from home. Being a good son and not wanting to see his mother left alone with his alcoholic father, Glenn is torn between pursuing his own goals and staying home to help stabilize the chaotic environment. His brothers and sisters are in their teens now and have never been exposed to their father at his worst. Glenn has always felt that he should shield them from knowing how bad it is. If he left home, who would fetch his father from the bar? Who would supplement the family's income? Worse yet, who would be a companion for his mother? She looks to Glenn to do the errands, the man's work around the house and talk to her whenever Glenn's father doesn't come home.

As if Glenn weren't concerned enough, his mother reminds him continually, "I don't know what I'd do if you weren't around to help me." Glenn's mother is also the daughter of an alcoholic who died without ever seeking help. To Lisa, it is normal to mold her life around an addict, taking responsibility for him and shoring him up. Subconsciously, the tradition has been passed on to Glenn and his brothers and sisters: the tradition of sacrificing your life and goals on the altar of a parent's inability to cope with life. Without admitting it to herself, she is subtly giving Glenn the message that it isn't O.K. to leave home, not now, maybe not ever, at least not until Glenn's father dies. Other family friends have picked up Glenn's mother's chorus, reminding him of how responsible he is and what her life would turn into if he left now.

So Glenn wonders when it would be O.K. to leave home. He sees no end in sight to his father's drinking and is unsure of his mother's ability to cope. He was on the verge of turning down the scholarship when he sought a counselor's advice.

Tradition's Hurting Power

Glenn has fallen into the trap that ensnares a great number of adults who come from dysfunctional homes—the inability to know when to leave home and feel good about it. Like other adult children, he is trying to remain in the home to save it from itself. Christian adult children have the added fear that if they leave the home, the parents or other siblings will not be able to accept Jesus Christ for want of a close Christian witness. Without realizing it they, like Glenn, have become tethered by the umbilical cord of codependency to their dysfunctional homes, which will become their emotional tombs unless they take the steps necessary to leave. Through counseling, Glenn found the courage to step out of his dysfunctional home environment and into God's will for his life. Here is what he learned that gave him the courage.

The Cocoon

As we have noted, the dysfunctional home tends to become a tomb. Rather than seeing the home as a stage of growth, the dysfunctional family regards the family as the end in itself. It is expected to remain static—problems, roles, traditions and all—and the energy of the family is heaped into keeping it static.

These binding traditions should be called into question. Why must we do it this way? And above all, what does God really want? The answer to the second question depends entirely on the individual's view of God, which is sometimes distorted because of his wounded soul. Thinking that God expects him to relinquish his comfortable boundaries can breed anger and resentment. The expectations of others are frequently meshed with God's. The result is guilt projection.

Thus, in order to be healed of the wounds and become a functioning member of God's Kingdom, it is sometimes necessary to escape the unhealthy confines of the dysfunctional home. In order to escape, you must deal effectively with issues of conscience and guilt.

The dysfunctional home is the principal incubator for the ways of the world. Its binding power threatens the very foundation of the Gospel, which is the Lordship of Christ. To the degree that the dysfunctional home dictates behavior, Jesus cannot assume the throne in the believer's life. He is controlled by another lord who uses parents and siblings and their beliefs and fears to trap the Christian into his mold, thwarting their effectiveness, not to mention their peace and joy. The home has become a tomb. But a simple change in perspective to God's way of thinking can bring freedom: *If your home is a tomb, see it as a cocoon.*

The cocoon is a place in which the caterpillar hibernates from outside elements while a transformation occurs. In fact, the Greek word for *transformation* in Romans 12:2 is the same word from which we derive the word *metamorphosis,* the process by which the body of the caterpillar changes into another completely different form, the butterfly. But one thing is certain: in the words of a newly formed butterfly, "If I'm going to fly, I've got to get out of here!"

In order to fly free, we must escape the confines of the cocoon and do what we were created and called of God to do. This transformation of the adult child has a parallel in the human birth process.

Life in Utero

While a developing baby is in the uterus, he is passing through stages of development which, if unhindered, will produce a child able to live outside the womb and develop further into a healthy adult.

But the child in utero in a dysfunctional home has a different experience. Dr. Mike Samuels and his wife, Nancy, authors of *The Well Pregnancy Book,* reveal that many of the dysfunctions we have mentioned in this book can have a significant negative influence on a baby's development. If the mother is poverty-stricken, the high stress and lack of nutritious foods rob the baby of proper stimulation and nourishment. The mother who uses alcohol or nicotine decreases her developing baby's ability to use nutrients while flooding his system with a toxic chemical. Mothers under severe emotional stress also restrict their developing babies' abilities to use nutrients. The mother who diets compulsively causes her baby's acidic levels to increase dangerously. The working mother subjects her baby to fatigue, stress and often nutritional neglect.

These factors and others result in low birth weight babies, premature babies, serious infant illnesses, miscarriages (not the only cause), stillbirth and reduced cell size. The life in the uterus of the mother can afford both benefit and harm to the growing baby, who helplessly and trustingly awaits the day of his birth.

The Dysfunctional Child Growing Up "in Utero"

The child growing up in a dysfunctional home is as affected by his surroundings as the human baby is in his mother's womb.

The stress of dysfunction in a home environment severely restricts the flow of emotional nurturing.

Take divorce as one example. According to psychologist Judith Wallerstein, "Almost one half of children of divorces enter adulthood as worried, underachieving, self-deprecating and sometimes angry young men and women." In her research conducted over a fifteen-year period with sixty families, including 131 children who were ages two through eighteen at the time of their parents' divorce, the following symptoms existed, among many others: Two-thirds of the girls who had seemingly sailed through the divorce suddenly became anxious as young adults, unable to make lasting commitments and fearful of betrayal in intimate relationships; many boys who were more overtly troubled in the post-divorce years failed to develop a sense of independence, confidence or purpose. They drifted in and out of college and from job to job. Three out of five of these children felt rejected by at least one parent.

With all the pain in a dysfunctional home, why is it so hard for these hurting adult children to leave—either physically or emotionally? In spite of all the difficulties in a dysfunctional home, it is still home and for many adult children there is no place like it. In some ways, it is like prison to which some convicts continually return because they fear facing life and responsibility. They have a planned life, a bed, scheduled work and amusement, food and company—not always good, but at least familiar. It is familiar and living there does not require developing a new coping strategy or breaking difficult traditions. It is easier to burrow back into the nest than live and breathe in independence.

This habit has a parallel in human birth. Although most full-term babies are born about 39 weeks after conception, there are always those procrastinators—little folks who just ignore the deadline. Grandmother's plane ticket has expired, and they are resting happily in the womb. But after 42 weeks a baby in utero can develop dysmaturity or postmaturity syndrome. Unless he exits the womb, the place that once afforded him nourishment and health can become destructive. Although babies born with this syndrome are able to maintain their head size and length, their appearance is that of a premature infant. Their skin is loose, dry and wrinkled. The fine hair that covers the bodies of other newborns is eaten away, and their skin, instead of the wholesome reddish-pink cast, is yellowish, stained by their own excrement. The placenta has given out, unable to furnish the proper nutrients and oxygen the baby needs. These babies who overstay their welcome run a greater risk of death before, during and after labor. They have medical problems similar to those of premature infants, including neurological handicapping.

What is the solution to the overripe unborn? According to doctors, induced labor. Whereas the normal infant knows when to initiate his birth, the postmature infant does not. His hypothalamus gland is not properly programmed to signal the onset of labor with a dramatic rise in estrogen levels. So this fellow just sits there waiting for circumstances beyond him to open up. The watchful eye of a skilled obstetrician quite literally rescues the infant from himself, sometimes with induced labor or a Caesarean section. Escaping the womb becomes essential to preserving his life.

So it is with the adult in a dysfunctional home. Like our little procrastinator in the uterus, this adult does not know when the time is right to separate from his environment. He cannot read the warning signs and does not know how to get things going or even if he has the right to do so. He has long since passed his "due" date, his debut into society. He is plagued with a desire to leave and a fear that if he leaves, somehow things might fall apart. It is the codependent's nightmare of indecision. If he is a Christian, he wants more than anything to know whether God approves of his moving into a new dimension, but his fears usually prevail and postpone the blessed event.

The Coming-Out Principle

Everyone needs a physical birthday, an emotional birthday and a spiritual birthday. The physical birthday happens the day we physically enter the world. The spiritual birthday happens the day we assume responsibility for our sins and trust Jesus Christ to save us. The emotional birthday is often postponed or ignored. This is the day we emerge from our homes, independent human beings ready to develop our own homes and assume responsibility for our mistakes and choices. The postponing of the emotional birthday is what makes adult children. They have stopped growing emotionally. The adult child is sometimes positively childlike, but very often childish as a result of emotional dysmaturity syndrome. He needs desperately to feel he has permission to shed the cocoon of his home and step into the next phase of life. In order to do this, he must pass through a crisis of conscience.

Our consciences are affected by the traditions of our homes, religious beliefs, social customs and other factors. In order for a person to step out of his home, his conscience must be clean. For the Christian to have a clean conscience, he must be assured that his steps are in the will of God. But he often equates this with the approval of his family. In a dysfunctional home, approval may be suddenly withdrawn. This throws doubt on whether or not it is really God's will. Therefore, it becomes doubly difficult to move. A conscience tinged with guilt combined with emotional wounds can stymie the onset of an emotional birth process. In order to understand God's view of this, let's look in the Scriptures at those who left home in the will of God.

It is a spiritual principle that separation usually precedes revelation—a greater understanding about God and His relationship to us. Had several Bible characters remained at home, they would have been irretrievably harmed by their circumstances. Separation from the negative influences of environment, including family, culture, religion and occupation, was often the only godly way of finding the will of God (2 Corinthians 6:14–18). While some advocate blooming where you're planted, it would be more correct to say, "Bloom where God plants you," and often that is far away from home.

Abraham, the father of the faithful and friend of God, was specifically told by God to get up from his kindred and his father's house if he would have a relationship with God and see the Promised Land. Rebekah had to leave home to marry Isaac. Joseph was squeezed out of his home by his brothers' cruelty and deceit, but he found the will of God in the land of Egypt. Moses couldn't deliver Israel sitting in a Bedouin's tent in Midian. The Israelites didn't take over the government of Egypt but left to find the Promised Land. Ruth didn't find happiness and restoration until she left her familiar Moab to go to Bethlehem with her mother-in-law. Esther had to leave home and Uncle Mordecai to become queen and rescue her people. David had to flee the house of his father-in-law Saul to escape violence and abuse. Jesus had to leave home to fulfill his role as Messiah, and the early Church was disseminated over the face of the earth through persecution, uprooted and placed like leaven in the different societies of the world.

Throughout the Bible, "Get thee up" is an established, divine principle that precedes the unveiling of the will of God in the believer's life. Leaving home in days when there were no phones or Federal Express meant severing ties and communication, and it was initially painful, but the reward was both temporal and eternal.

Labor and Delivery

When a person comes to Jesus Christ and experiences a total change in lifestyle that accompanies salvation, he is sometimes dismayed to find that his household does not approve of his new-found faith. He is held up for ridicule and verbal abuse and finds himself a source of irritation. He is tempted to quarrel with those he most wants to influence for Christ. Some family members attempt purposely to harass him into stumbling—sometimes successfully. If he has been an addict, his old friends and relatives can play into his addictive behavioral patterns and increase his chances of lapsing back into bondage to the addictive cycle. The one who wants to follow Jesus, the Prince of Peace, suddenly finds himself embroiled in emotional conflict with those closest to him.

What is happening is a series of events designed to expel the adult child from the security he has always called home. Like the full-term baby, too closely cramped by the limitations of his mother, the adult child begins to feel the big squeeze. The emotional conflicts he feels are labor pains, which make way for the baby to emerge into a full-fledged, independent life. No wonder teenagers have such conflict at home. Their emotions are beginning to signal that it's going to be time to leave in a few short years, much like the baby's hypothalamus gland signals the mother's body to begin labor.

During labor, contraction after contraction opens the door of the cervix for the baby to enter the world. Several steps can trigger the onset of labor and delivery from the dysfunctional home. Your decision to implement these steps will undoubtedly precipitate conflict. So hold onto your hypothalamus and let's go.

Contraction #1

Refuse to play the games.

We have already discussed in chapters 3 and 4 the peculiar traits, traditions and roles played out in a dysfunctional home. But what would happen if you refused to play by its rules? What if instead of maintaining the tradition of silence, you started talking about the family's wounds and the fact that they could be healed? What if you flew in the face of tradition and declared that you had a plan for life other than minding the family store like your father, grandfather and great-grandpa before him? What if you refused to be the "carrier pigeon" for messages or stopped placating and caretaking? What if you let a few people suffer the consequences for their irresponsible behavior instead of covering for them? I'll tell you what would happen. Pandemonium would—will—break loose. You will feel the squeeze of a lot of guilt projection, but it's only natural. They have their ways and probably won't change. But then, since you know what your conscience wants, neither will you. A parting of the ways is imminent.

Contraction #2

Set your boundaries.

Wouldn't it be wonderful to say no to the family's expectations and feel good about it? You can do this when you know in your heart that it is the right thing to do. Adult children are usually led by their wounded souls, however, which causes them to be unsure of themselves. It is good to know that Jesus Christ set boundaries around Himself to protect His relationships with God and with His disciples. He wasn't anybody's doormat. He was in control of what He wanted to do and was God-led, not need-led.

The adult who is not in control, but has relinquished that authority over his life to others, is like a city without walls. He is usually angry and bitter about what others are doing to him. Try saying no a few times when unrealistic expectations are placed on you as an adult child and be prepared for another squeeze.

Contraction #3

Face your fears.

The fear of man is the binding fear that holds a person out of the will of God. You cannot say no to those you fear because you might lose their approval. Even Jesus had enemies and the Bible says not having any is bad for you. You will always make some enemies when you are doing the will of God and making and taking responsibility for the outcome of your choices.

The fear of failure is another fear that keeps the adult child bound to the womb. What if I get out there and need financial support? What if I can't find the right job? What if . . . ? So what? Fail and get it over with and get on with living. The truth is that you will fail many times, but you will never know what you could have done until you try.

When fear is avoided continually, it controls; when it is faced, it is defeated. God is holding your hand throughout this labor and delivery. There is nothing to fear that He cannot handle.

Contraction #4

Refuse to allow yourself to be controlled or abused.

The victimizer in the dysfunctional home has always looked for a victim and has found it in you. Now, when you have nothing to fear and have set your boundaries in place, you can expect his full fury. By this time, you are moving into a phase of labor comparable to a mother's transition phase, the most active part of labor. It is not unusual for the mother to get irritable with those around her because her contractions are so intense and every fiber of her being is concentrating on cooperating with the labor process. At the first infraction of your boundaries, be prepared to carry out any threats you have made.

Delivery

Take a calculated, carefully planned look and dive out headfirst.

Notice that the head comes first in normal deliveries; we can't get too far without it. The adult child needs his head on straight if he is to make a successful break with his family and begin his life in a new dimension. Dysfunctional adult children often lead with their wounds rather than their heads and the result is a mess. You cannot afford to feel guilt over the wake of debris left in the background. It will gnaw at your conscience and try to pull you back.

Change locations. Get a new job. Enroll in college. Go ahead and marry your sweetheart—especially if he/she is a healthy person and ready to separate from his/her own home cocoon and fly. As you pray and knock, the doors will open for you. Keep trying. Some births take hours in the delivery room. Do not be dissuaded by setbacks. Continue your plans to achieve and maintain freedom and your right to be an adult.

Severing the Umbilical Cord

Once you are out of your environment, it may be necessary to sever an umbilical cord that tethers you emotionally to your home.

Through this invisible cord travel guilt and the binding power of traditions. Don't respond to projected guilt. Continue gently but firmly to say no. Recognize that the plans and goals for your life are as important as theirs. Traditions can sometimes have a binding effect in sentimental moments, but be careful lest your sentimentality draw you back to the old womb. Make a clean cut and it will heal faster. Nurturing, no matter how dysfunctional, has always come through this cord. Now you will have to look to God for that nurturing and care. You will have to learn to walk in the Spirit and take responsibility for your decisions and choices.

Once it is done, give yourself a few choruses of "Happy Birthday," celebrate with friends and get on with life.

And, by the way, resist the urge to worry about the folks back home. Almost every mother recovers from natural labor and delivery to lead a productive, normal life, even repeating this process several times. In my own case, I cannot remember what a labor pain actually feels like, although I delivered two babies, eight- and ten-pounders, without medication.

When You Cannot Escape Immediately

The solution above is for a majority of adult children who have never left home emotionally. But what about the wife or husband who is in an abusive situation—living with an alcoholic or a physical abuser or a person with some other major dysfunction that makes life miserable? Should you leave your husband/wife/children/job to escape evil? It depends on the type of evil. If your spouse is abusing you and the children physically, committing incest, involved in adulterous habit patterns, endangering you and your family legally and morally with drug addiction or biologically with homosexuality, by all means, get thee up. But some situations are not so simple. Not all evil needs to be fled. Some less critical situations are in our lives for redemptive reasons, which we cannot see immediately. If it is God's will for you to endure, He will give you the grace to survive and thrive in those circumstances.

Several times while writing this book, I have felt the urge to write under chapter headings, "Read such-and-such a book!" One is a must-read on my list—especially for Christians. It's Dr. James Dobson's *Love Must Be Tough*. The word *codependency* was not even popular when this champion of the family wrote about the subject, and I applaud his courage; we needed some cold water in our faces to wake us up.

Dr. Dobson believes that there are cases of family dysfunction in which a spouse must initiate and precipitate a crisis that will threaten the marriage bond. One of those is repeated marital unfaithfulness. Writes Dobson,

> At the appropriate moment and armed with prayer . . . I would urge her to precipitate a crisis of major proportions. She must give [her unfaithful husband] a reason for wanting to reroute his river. . . . He is unlikely to make the invest-ment of energy and self-control to accomplish that task until he absolutely must. It is only when he becomes mis-erable that he will accept the responsibility for change. It is only when he sees everything of value to him—his home, his children, his wife, his reputation—begin to slip away that his choices will become clear. It is only when the well runs dry that [he] will begin to miss the water.

Dobson is speaking not only to wives, but husbands as well who find themselves in similar circumstances. He is talking about a sequence of events similar to those in our "labor process."

Please understand that you must choose your course of action based on your circumstances, the will of God determined by prayer, sound counsel and advice, and your own conscience.

Such crises must not be taken lightly because they could lead to the dissolution of your marriage or of other relationships you hold dear. The cost of remaining must be weighed carefully against the cost of separation. If you leave, you must make preparation and plan your confrontation carefully so that its effects will be maximized. You may have only one chance.

Janice's Story

Janice shared with me how leaving her parents' home made the difference in her spiritual walk.

Janice had a very dysfunctional home of origin. Her father was a "bottom-of-the-line alcoholic" who had been kicked out of their home for his drinking when Janice was a small child. She never saw him again until she was 26 years old. Shortly after she saw him he died from alcoholism, his brain so deteriorated that he couldn't hold a thought.

Janice's early years were spent in poverty in a housing project. When Janice was ten her mother married a man who was fifteen years older than her mother and financially secure, able to give them the home they longed for. He had swept Janice's mother off her feet, but immediately after marrying her, he made a complete personality reversal, turning into a selfish, angry man.

Under this stress, Janice's mother turned to alcohol, creating more dysfunction in an already stressful marriage. To keep things from falling apart, Janice assumed the mother's role—cooking, cleaning, sewing, caretaking for a family that couldn't function normally.

In spite of her efforts, her stepfather, a workaholic and food addict, had little time for her. Janice recalls one painful incident among many. She cut her foot on a rusty pipe. As it bled profusely her stepfather left her home alone saying, "Your mother will take care of it." But Janice's mother didn't come home for eight more hours.

There was constant fighting. Her mother berated her stepfather and he responded in explosive anger.

When Janice was eighteen, she met Jesus Christ and committed herself to following as closely to the Lord as possible. It was through prayer and Bible reading that she began to understand her need to escape her dysfunctional home. "I spent practically the whole summer the year after I came to the Lord in prayer," says Janice. During this time of seeking God's will, she heard Him say: *Janice, leave home or it will destroy you.* As she began to pray toward that end, the Lord opened up an apartment within 24 hours and supplied the funds. It happened so quickly that Janice was able to make a sudden, clean break with her past.

She noticed immediately a significant difference in her attitude. "You can't be objective in a dysfunctional home because of the control and the shame. They have such a control on your mind." After leaving she would return home for brief visits, but was no longer affected emotionally. To Janice it was like watching a movie.

At one point her objectivity and determination caused her to break the tradition of silence about her family's dysfunctional behavior. An argument ensued. Janice apologized for hurting their feelings, but her parents refused to let it go. This time as she went out onto the porch to regain her composure, she began to pray. The Lord assured her of His continued love and forgiveness and showed her that the problem was theirs—not hers. The guilt and condemnation she had fallen victim to so quickly before leaving home no longer held the rein of her emotions. Her soul was being restored.

But something else happened as a result of Janice's decision to leave home. One of Janice's main reasons for trying to stay home had been the hope that she would be able to influence her mother to receive Jesus Christ as her Lord and Savior. Janice had prayed often for this, but to no avail. Plus she had often felt frustrated by "blowing" her Christian witness in the trials of her home environment.

As we see in Figure 4 on page 34, it sometimes happens that when a codependent leaves the confines of the dysfunctional home and severs the umbilical cord of control, the problem person, who is often not a Christian, finds himself in a position of needing help. Janice's mother began to take Janice's Christian witness seriously after Janice left home. Not only that, but God set other laborers around her mother to help harvest her for God's Kingdom. Janice's mother has since become a Christian. Janice never regrets leaving home when she did and sees now that it was a necessary step in her spiritual growth, as well as a key to her mother's salvation. She was able to let go and let Jesus save her mother.

When an adult child steps out into a new dimension you might wonder if things get better immediately. That depends, as we will see in the next chapter.

6
Facing the Damage

Anyone who has grown up in a dysfunctional home is often unaware of how deeply he was affected by his environment. Take a pencil and answer the following questions to determine if you have sustained emotional damage from that experience.

Beside each number choose the letter of the response that most accurately reflects the truth about you:

a. frequently
b. sometimes
c. seldom

_____ 1. Do you have difficulty sustaining feelings of joy?

_____ 2. Do you have trouble *feeling* that God loves you, and sensing His presence?

_____ 3. When disappointments come, do you fight feeling angry with God?

_____ 4. Are you often numb emotionally, unable to feel things very deeply?

_____ 5. Do you have difficulty taking changes in stride?

_____ 6. Do you resent the help of those who "haven't been there"?

_____ 7. Are you easily or frequently depressed?

_____ 8. When you read the Bible do you feel God's Word is condemning you?

_____ 9. Are most of your close friends from dysfunctional homes?

_____ 10. Yes or no: Did you marry or do you gravitate toward persons of the opposite sex who are children of dysfunctional homes or who are compulsive-addictive persons themselves?

_____ 11. Do you have a habit of letting people down at the last minute, failing to fulfill obligations, commitments, promises and responsibilities?

_____ 12. Do you manifest any of the dysfunctional roles in your current family or other relationships (martyr, hero, lost child, placater, clown, scapegoat)?

_____ 13. Are you subject to emotional roller coaster rides, fluctuating between elation and self-pity?

_____ 14. Do you tend to be serious-minded, finding little humor in your mistakes?

_____ 15. Do you have trouble expressing your emotions to others and to God?

_____ 16. Yes or no: Are you afraid to look at your past?

_____ 17. Yes or no: Did you marry young to escape a dysfunctional environment or prolong the decision to marry out of fear?

_____ 18. Do you disguise your anger with a mask of politeness and happiness?

_____ 19. Do you have difficulty making long-term commitments to others because you are unable to trust them?

_____ 20. Do you feel the need to rescue people from situations and problems or to come up with help and solutions for them?

_____ 21. Do you feel the need for authority figures' approval?

_____ 22. Are you overly inclined to introspection?

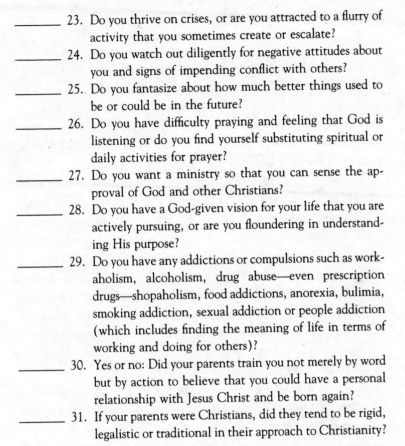

_____ 23. Do you thrive on crises, or are you attracted to a flurry of activity that you sometimes create or escalate?

_____ 24. Do you watch out diligently for negative attitudes about you and signs of impending conflict with others?

_____ 25. Do you fantasize about how much better things used to be or could be in the future?

_____ 26. Do you have difficulty praying and feeling that God is listening or do you find yourself substituting spiritual or daily activities for prayer?

_____ 27. Do you want a ministry so that you can sense the approval of God and other Christians?

_____ 28. Do you have a God-given vision for your life that you are actively pursuing, or are you floundering in understanding His purpose?

_____ 29. Do you have any addictions or compulsions such as workaholism, alcoholism, drug abuse—even prescription drugs—shopaholism, food addictions, anorexia, bulimia, smoking addiction, sexual addiction or people addiction (which includes finding the meaning of life in terms of working and doing for others)?

_____ 30. Yes or no: Did your parents train you not merely by word but by action to believe that you could have a personal relationship with Jesus Christ and be born again?

_____ 31. If your parents were Christians, did they tend to be rigid, legalistic or traditional in their approach to Christianity?

Score: No one test can offer conclusive evidence, but if you answered _yes_ to 10 and 16, _no_ to 30 and/or answered as many as twelve with either _a, frequently,_ or _b, sometimes,_ this is a pretty good indication that the emotional damage you sustain is substantial. If you answered as many as eight with _a_ or _b,_ the amount of emotional damage could be moderate. Any _a_ or _b_ answers, however, should be made a matter of prayer because God wants you to be healed of these problems.

The One Out of Ten

When adult children come to church, they have often already accepted Jesus Christ. But what about the painful damage done to them by their living their whole lives in an atmosphere full of sin and death? For them to be cleansed from sin but to have to cope with wounds of the past is hardly the state in which Jesus prefers them to live.

The adult child may sincerely believe that he is already completely restored. Both an ignorance of what is normal in family relationships and how much he was affected by his former environment conspire together to keep him in his emotionally "deformed" condition. The newly emerging adult child has undergone the prelude to transformation, having the new spirit of Christ placed within him and shedding the cocoon of his past, but in order to be fully healed and restored, he needs to admit his need for another touch from God. His condition is very similar to the lepers that Jesus healed.

Of all the tragedies that encountered the people of Jesus' day, leprosy was the most insidious. One day a spot might appear on an outer extremity, perhaps an earlobe or a finger. Once it took hold in the extremities, the flesh would begin to rot in a matter of days. Leprosy struck indiscriminately—fathers, mothers, children. In fact, its capricious ability to strike at random caused it to be called *leprosy*, which means "a smiting." There was no known cure.

According to the Law of Moses, the disease of leprosy rendered a person permanently unclean unless, by God's mercy, he was somehow healed. Anyone found carrying the disease had to be isolated immediately, forced outside the city walls, placed in a leper colony. To live for years apart from friends and family, never able to touch those you loved, to see them only at a distance and to have to warn others not to come near you had devastating emotional effects as well.

A few cases of cleansing were recorded in the Old Testament: to Miriam, who was healed by Moses' prayer, and Naaman, the Syrian, who sought out the prophet Elisha and washed in the Jordan. But even if the spread of the disease were checked and the sores disappeared, the irreversible emotional damage had been done and no one could restore it—that is, until Jesus.

When Jesus performed the first few healings, word traveled fast. Thus, when Jesus, en route to Jerusalem, entered a small village between Samaria and Galilee, a group of ten lepers confronted Him at a distance and cried out for His mercy.

Without touching them, He commanded them to go and show themselves to the priests. As they made their way to the synagogue, their spots were cleansed and the progress of the disease was permanently and visibly halted.

One of the ten, a Samaritan, was so overwhelmed with joy and thanksgiving that he returned to worship Jesus and, falling at His feet, he began to thank Him for the miracle that would restore him to his family. Jesus mourned the fact that the other nine had not thought to give thanks but, turning to the one, said, "Go your way, your faith has made you well." What He really said to the man was, "Your faith has now healed you emotionally." With a word, Jesus restored what the leprosy had eaten away so that not only was the man's body cleansed, but his body and mind were also made whole as though the horrifying disease had never happened.

Once adult children have emerged from the atmospheres of their dysfunctional homes, they usually appear in the condition illustrated by Figure 4 on page 34. Like the nine lepers, they are cleansed of their "leprosy." They have emerged from the cocoon of the dysfunctional home and are venturing out to explore their relationships with Jesus Christ and find functional people with whom to replace the dysfunctional relationships of the past. They have found a measure of freedom, but are still misshapen by the molds of their dysfunctional homes. Like the lepers, they are cleansed, but not yet fully restored.

The result is that they often have difficulty fitting into an environment—including the church environment—in which the traditions, habits and roles of the dysfunctional home are unacceptable coping strategies. Manipulation doesn't work with people who want to be direct. Triangling doesn't work when you can't find a carrier pigeon for your messages. Silence doesn't work if you want to be around people who talk about how they feel.

What sometimes happens, though, is that a large number of children from dysfunctional homes will all find their way to the same church usually because of the fact that they are alike. Without realizing it, the congregation full of scarred and crippled members begins to operate like a dysfunctional home. In almost every local church, you will find a mixture of healthy and unhealthy people trying to develop relationships with each other. The results can be a disastrous breeding of internal conflict unless the members become aware of what is happening and change.

The dysfunctional church sometimes spends more time healing itself than it does in serving Jesus Christ. I believe the ministry of the church must involve both the healing of its own body and the flow of healing to society, but the outflow is hindered unless there is healing and restoration within.

The answer for the dysfunctional church, as it was for the leper Jesus restored, is the healing, body, soul and spirit, of every individual member so that we can enjoy our relationship with

God, love one another in a godly way and not just tell, but show the world about Jesus Christ.

A huge barrier usually stands in the way of the wounded adult child recovering from his wounds: denial that any damage has been done.

Let's explore it.

Denial of Any Damage

Believe it or not, Christian adult children develop some positive traits in their dysfunctional homes that can carry them through life if, necessary. As a result of coping with their environments, they can survive almost anything—financial stress, persecution for their faith, church splits, the rigors of the mission field. Because of their own deprivation, they want to share the love that now fills their hearts because of Jesus Christ's presence. They want to help others because they are sensitized to the problems commonly shared by those who have walked through trouble. They are effective crisis managers who can stand through a storm of criticism without flinching.

All of these are good traits and can strengthen anyone who is ministry-minded. But there is a catch. These tendencies can cause problems, too. Without realizing it, adult children will substitute these traits for the working of the fruit of the Holy Spirit.

In the struggle to be as normal as everyone else and somehow to escape the shame of the past, the Christian adult child tends to deny or minimize the presence of emotional damage. Thus he sees self-promotion that seems to bear fruit as the work of God. He confuses the voice of inner coping mechanisms with the voice of the Holy Spirit. This is complicated by being out of the confines of his dysfunctional environment. Because he doesn't feel bound, he thinks he isn't. What he is denying, though, is the shape or the "misshape" he is in and his need to be conformed to the image of Christ.

This conformity does not happen overnight with a salvation experience or any other spiritual experience. Compulsive people always desire quick solutions to problems. Perhaps this is why the miraculous claims of the Gospel attract the hurting. We tend to think: If I could just get the right minister to pray for me all my problems would disappear. If I could find the magic key in Scripture that would unlock the door, I would find complete healing. If I could only sing "He Touched Me" enough times, I would be released. If the people around me would only get saved, or get more of God, my problems would be over.

In *Leaving the Enchanted Forest: The Path from Relationship Addiction to Intimacy*, authors Stephanie Covington and Liana Beckett say it this way: "Children who were raised in dysfunctional homes often grow up in a wounded child state. And, as adults, the sense of deprivation is so deeply buried, its insistent call often goes unrecognized. Instead, people seek quick emotional fixes that drown it out." The quick emotional fixes include addictions and compulsions.

The truth is that emotional catharsis does not equal a touch from God, nor does it last. It may bring a needed emotional discharge, but it cannot be construed as the permanent answer or substitute for the gradual renewing of the mind that alone affects lasting transformation. After every experience or insight, we need desperately to be aware of what actually happened to us and what remains to be healed. Otherwise, an emotional impact of spiritual insight and revelation propels us into thinking that this experience was all we needed. We tend to exaggerate the impact of that one revelation or touch from God.

To use another example from Scripture, we might relate this to the blind man who was healed by the Lord Jesus Christ. Having been brought to Jesus to have his sight restored, he received a touch from Jesus.

"What do you see?" asked Jesus.

"I see men like trees walking!" was his honest reply. In response, Jesus reached out and touched him again. "Now I see all men clearly!" cried the once-blind man.

But what if the blind man had pretended to be perfectly whole after the first touch? Jesus told the Pharisees, "Because you say 'we see,' your sin remains." What we often do is rush out of the presence of God with a distorted view. We need to wait for the second touch to put our experiences into perspective and allow our spiritual eyes time to focus.

The person who has received an initial touch from God tends to believe that all is taken care of, under the blood, in the past. His immediate feelings may deny the presence of emotional damage, but as he stumbles through the Christian life and encounters difficulty in relationships with others, and the presence of addictions and compulsions, he sometimes has to admit that he needs either a new pair of glasses or another touch from God.

Whether or not we come from dysfunctional homes, we all need renewing of our minds because all of us have been damaged emotionally by some aspect of our pasts. This is the age-old process at work known as sanctification, conforming us to the image of Jesus Christ. To deny that we need this stunts our Christian growth and to believe that it occurs in one experience is shortsighted.

What shatters denial? The hammer of truth. Whereas we were once cloistered in deception or inaccurate perception, suddenly the light comes crashing in and we understand things from God's perspective. But how does truth invade a darkened understanding?

Denial is the emotional defense mechanism that enables us to face crises without breaking down emotionally. Facing the emotional impact of the truth is postponed temporarily so that one's thinking can remain clear. But denial is normally only a stage. It gives way eventually to the other stages of grief: emotional anguish, anger, depression, hope and resolution.

The child brought up in a dysfunctional home, in order to cope emotionally with his tragedy and hurt, operates continually in this state of mind. He pretends that nothing is wrong for so long that his emotions shut down. He never moves into the final stages of grief and, thus, never finds resolution and emotional healing.

You can generally tell you are around a person in denial because you are afraid to tell him or her the truth. This is uncomfortable for an honest person. He has to lie himself to remain loyal and friendly and to placate the person who is denying unpleasant realities. Like the emperor in the fairy tale, the person who is in denial believes he is clothed when he is really naked and is surrounded frequently by people who help hold up his invisible train. Each is afraid to admit the truth for fear of facing a reality that the person is unprepared emotionally to handle.

It takes the interjection of an honest person to help him face reality. Faithful are the wounds of a friend who, in love, is not afraid to speak the truth.

If you suspect you are in denial, the three steps that follow will help you find release. The first will help you take an honest look at why you do the things you do.

Admitting the Damage Done

The first step in breaking denial and moving on in the healing process is admitting damage has occurred. Some are able to admit this partially but deny the extent of it. Both must be recognized if denial is to shatter. One way to start is to consider the results of the quiz you took at the beginning of this chapter. If you were honest about the answers, your score should give you some idea of your need for healing.

In *Grown-Up Abused Children,* authors James Leehan and Laura P. Wilson describe five major recurring problems that hinder or prevent the abused child from functioning as a happy, healthy, productive individual. They are: "1) a basic sense of mistrust toward self and others and a consequent inability to establish deep meaningful interpersonal and sexual relationships; 2) deeply ingrained feelings of low self-worth which are frequently reflected in disparaging self-statements and the belief that 'no one could possibly care about me because I'm not worth it'; 3) lack of expertise in basic social skills which further impedes the ability to establish friendships and other relationships; 4) a sense of helplessness which frequently results in an inability to make decisions and is manifested in many lives by haphazard, seemingly unplanned life goals and events; 5) difficulty in identifying, acknowledging and disclosing feelings, especially evident in the underlying, frequently debilitating feelings of anger, guilt and depression."

Do any of these sound familiar to you? It can be hard to admit it, but you must be willing to believe there is a reason behind these behaviors. It takes courage, as do the next steps, but it is the only way to break the denial.

I know a couple, both abused as children, who deny the extent of their problems and the effect these have on their ability to establish and maintain relationships. This denial keeps them from the healing they so desperately need. Like whipped dogs, they both shy away when anyone—especially an authority figure—gets too close. They cannot seek counseling for fear of damaging their reputations and their chances at a ministry. If those around them don't "hold up their invisible train," they abandon them, repeating the abandonment they experienced growing up. If they cannot admit that their unresolved grief and anger affects the present and will affect the future, they will continue to have difficulties and never understand why.

Admitting the Need for Help

Perhaps you, like this couple, need to take the second step in breaking denial. After first admitting the extent of the damage done, you need to admit that the "first touch" was inadequate to bring clear understanding and complete healing to your problems. In other words, you need help.

In the past, if this couple came for prayer, Bill and I would have spent hours ministering to them and praying with them. If problems had continued to surface, I wouldn't have wanted to know for fear that I was not a good enough pastor. I perceived my role as pinpointing the answer to each problem. The more problems that arose, the more inadequate I felt when I could not find the answers. It was necessary for me to resolve my own issues of codependency in order to recommend that some of our parishioners needed counseling beyond what we could give. "Soaking" prayer did initiate the healing process and bring relief to many people—and this coupled with an honest evaluation of your situation may bring about the healing you need. If the pain or denial persists, however, you may need to consider the help a counselor can provide. The couple I mentioned need long-term counseling by a Christian psychotherapist if their problems are to be resolved. Counseling like that requires not only a knowledge of God's ways, but the intricate knowledge of human nature and the expertise to draw out the issues that lead to healing.

I believe that the secular study of human behavior is extremely valuable to help us understand the way mankind, the crown of God's creation, responds to his fallen environment. We are only beginning to understand the intricacies of the human mind, but even the little we know is valuable in matters of spiritual discernment because it helps us separate those thoughts and actions that are man-inspired from those that are God-inspired. God has mercifully built into the human soul a resiliency much like that found in the physical body. Anyone, therefore, is capable of bouncing back from some of the worst experiences to attain a measure of happiness and peace. If this were not so, we would die from our emotional wounds.

But as helpful as the study of human behavior is, it has a limitation. The secular psychologist has an intricate knowledge of the first Adam, the fallen creation, but he lacks what the Holy Spirit can provide: not only insight but transformation. Many secular self-help books recommend various new coping strategies for emotional wounds, but their prescriptions usually fall miserably short of complete healing. Because they do not take into account the last Adam, Jesus Christ, they cannot offer full restoration. In preparation for writing this book, I saw this frequently in a multitude of non-Christian self-help books. The promised prescriptions seldom went far enough. They left me dangling—understanding problems in depth, giving me a greater handle on the behavior of those I read about in Scripture, but shedding little light on solutions. The solutions that were offered were usually for the benefit of one's own perceived happiness, as though human happiness were the end in itself.

And in all fairness, traditional Christianity can approach the healing of the soul with applications of Scripture that are sometimes out of context and by giving an incomplete picture because it neglects the psychologist's intricate knowledge of the first

Adam. Christians know, for example, that mankind's root problem is sin, but we don't know how those sins specifically affect behavioral patterns. If we applied this to "worldly" understanding, perhaps we could discern what we are seeing and how better to apply the healing balm of Jesus Christ to the wounded.

I believe that the Church has something to learn about God's desire for our happiness and the healing of our emotions. But God has a higher interest in our restoration, the development of the image of Jesus Christ in each of His children. This process is not only for our happiness, but for our highest good and culminates in the redemption of our souls. When human behavioral patterns are discovered in Scripture and we see their problems resolved in its pages, we derive the maximum benefit from the information provided by the secular psychologist.

I no longer feel guilty when it is time to refer parishioners out for counseling. I am relieved that God has called other ministries to stand behind the pastor and help heal the members of the Body of Christ. The counseling ministry affords a place where those who need long-term expert help can receive it. Sometimes people need to hear what pastors are saying to them from another source before they will believe it. When money is paid for counseling, even Christians are more likely to follow the advice given! If you are having trouble breaking denial, you may want to make an appointment with your pastor or a trained professional counselor for insight into your problem.

In addition, a third step must be taken if healing is to be forthcoming: overcoming the fear of change.

Overcoming the Fear of Change

Not only does denial follow the adult child into the church and thwart his complete healing, but rigidity, the unwillingness to change, prevents even the soundest counsel and the most powerful ministry from being beneficial. James 1:22 says, "Prove yourselves doers of the word, and not merely hearers who delude themselves." No prescription for help whether through prayer, Bible study, counseling or the Twelve Step program will work for anyone who is not ready to effect change in his life.

Jesus' ministry was rejected by the scribes and Pharisees but devoured hungrily by multitudes who were ready to receive His healing actions and words. Almost all of us act like Pharisees sometimes, preferring tradition over change.

The following chapters in this book can benefit you if you are ready to apply them to your life, but will be only wasted seed unless your heart is plowed up and ready to receive it. In fact, months or years later, some of these words may settle into your soul and you may be ready to receive truths you once rejected as being irrelevant to your life. And it will mean change.

Wayne Kritsberg, certified addiction counselor and author of *The Adult Children of Alcoholics Syndrome: From Discovery to Recovery*, sees three components necessary for the adult child of the dysfunctional home to be healed: 1) Emotional discharge; 2) Cognitive reconstruction; and 3) Behavioral action. Elaborating on this prescription he writes:

> It is important to restate that the above three components of recovery must be interactive for recovery to progress in a balanced way. An [adult child of an alcoholic] who just focuses on behavioral action runs the risk of continuing to stuff feelings, and remains with a negative outlook on life. Those who work only on emotional discharge often get caught in reliving emotional crises again and again, without really letting go of the emotional pain. They continue to remain in relationships that are sick and harmful, and

their outlook on life really does not change. Those who just work on being positive . . . repress emotions and smile a lot, even though they are in emotional pain. They often remain in destructive situations, and try to think their way out of them.

The traditions that control the adult child coming out of his dysfunctional environment have the capacity to bind him to the tomb of his past and compel him to repeat the dysfunctional behaviors of his parents. Emotional discharge, letting out the feelings and words you have so wanted to say about your pain, begins to break denial about the extent of emotional damage and eases the pressure within.

Cognitive reconstruction is what Ezekiel called "observing the sins of his father." To study with insight into human nature and with spiritual understanding the mistakes and the generational traditions of your family causes you to identify problems that have bound your family members for years.

Behavioral action is the second half of Ezekiel's prescription for breaking the curse: "not doing likewise." In other words, behavioral action means modifying your behavior to change the dysfunctional habits, traditions and roles and replacing them with godly ones.

Now that we are breaking denial and facing the damage, let's examine the specific emotional wounds that affect the spiritual life of the adult child and what it takes to heal them.

7
Restoring the Wounded Soul

Sonny was a purebred Afghan hound given to my sister-in-law, Susan, by a family who knew nothing of the treasure the dog could have been. Although a curtain remained over his past, any loud sounds or voices drove him into a panic. Susan quickly surmised that the dog had been subjected to abuse. His coat, the color of light sand, was drab and matted and his body bruised.

Susan, who is particularly talented in training animals, took him into her apartment, gave him his new name and worked with him patiently. Through her talents for working with dogs Sonny was completely restored physically to the fine specimen he was born to be. Although Sonny was loyal to Susan, he never lost his fear of loud noises. His physical condition was healed with his improved circumstances, but Sonny bore the effects of his abuse in his noble soul until the day he died. All Susan's efforts could only partially erase his wounds. Trusting human beings never came easily for him. He had been scarred so deeply that he never could let himself go completely and be loved and enjoy the pats of the rest of us who longed to touch him.

Like Sonny, Christians who are rescued from their troubled lives also bear the deep wounds inflicted on them by cruel, Satan-controlled people. Entombed in dysfunctional families, squeezed into abnormal molds and left to limp through life debilitated emotionally, these hurting people come to the Church for help. Once there, however, they often fail to find one of Jesus' primary ministries in operation: the healing of the brokenhearted. One of the most important aspects of restoration is usually all but ignored, the restoring of the soul. The Church is only now beginning to understand the need to recover not only spiritually, but emotionally as well.

What It Feels Like to Be Lost

Were you ever lost in a store as a child, separated from your parents, or as an adult lost in strange surroundings or stranded without hope of being easily or quickly found? My own daughter at age five was lost for several hours in suburban Washington, D.C. My cousin Nancy, who had asked to watch Sarah for the day, had driven to a friend's house to visit and let Sarah play in the yard with other children. But a while later when my cousin looked out, Sarah was gone.

When the other children left to go home, Sarah had forgotten which house to return to. She began to run up and down strange streets hoping to catch a glimpse of the car or some familiar landmark. Not finding any, she began to cry, feeling angry and frustrated with herself for being lost. Thoughts of fear began to flood her tiny heart. *What if they never come and find me? What will I do?* By this time she was walking down a highway only two blocks from the house where my cousin was, but as far as Sarah was concerned, miles away. Frightened and bewildered, Sarah began to pray, "Jesus, help me, I'm lost." As she ran, walked, cried and prayed, a man driving down the highway spotted her. Sensing something was wrong, he stopped, drove her to his home and called the police. Sarah was delighted when after only a few more minutes, Nancy pulled up at the man's house. To hear Sarah talk about the experience of being lost—now more than ten years ago—she seems not to carry an emotional scar. "I prayed, so there was nothing to worry about. I knew Jesus would take care of me." She never has been ruled by fear.

But my reaction is different. To realize that my daughter was lost in the suburb of the nation's crime capital, that a strange man picked her up in a car and took her to his house, that a thousand terrible endings could have come out of this story, causes emotions to rise that are difficult to handle.

Sarah was lost for a couple of hours, but what happens to a person who is lost for years? When someone is lost from God, we cannot think that years of roaming alone produces a healthy individual. The same emotions of panic, fear, anger and frustration that a small, lost child feels will be buried in his heart. He will likely have a sense of futility about living, a fear of dying, the sense of being abandoned and alone, waiting for something but not knowing when or what to expect. How often have Christian testimonies begun with these words: "My life had no meaning" or "I was searching for something"?

In order to deal effectively with the emotional impact of our lostness, a person learns to cope in thousands of different ways. All of these ways produce denial, swallowing fear, callousing ourselves against the realities of life, building walls against individuals to keep hurts away and turning to other things for distraction instead of facing what is really missing in our lives—a relationship with God the Father.

And when he finds that relationship, he needs to open himself to the fullness of restoration.

I have noticed that the following emotional difficulties affect the spiritual lives of Christians most directly.

1) Low self-esteem. This is a person's inability to see himself as lovable by God and others, remaining, therefore, unworthy of redemption and restoration. It masquerades as humility, but is actually a major factor in a person's disobeying God and retreating from others.

2) Fear of abandonment. The fear that God and others will leave him and that in the end he will be left alone to fend for himself produces hypervigilance, the tendency to look continually for danger in circumstances and relationships. Like any other fear, the fear of abandonment can manipulate a person into compromise, which is the fear of man. This is the root of all fears that keep a person from trusting God.

3) Perfectionism. This is the core belief that because of imperfection he must work to earn and maintain the approval of God or others. This is the basis for every idolatrous religion in the world and is even entangled in the emotions of many born-again Christians. Perfectionism creates all-or-nothing thinking and keeps a person from receiving and giving grace to others. The perfectionist demands seldom-attainable standards from others and himself, setting himself up for continual failure.

4) Authority problems. Rebellion against authority is the natural outflow of the fearful life, the thought life of the person who deeply believes that God does not have his best interests at heart and cannot, therefore, protect him from others who will take advantage of him. Unless the person is healed, he cannot become an integral, productive part of a local church or be happy

in his job or in any other environment where teamwork is necessary.

5) Shame. This is the emotion a person feels when vulnerable involuntarily, the emotion Adam and Eve felt immediately when they recognized they were naked. It is one of the core emotions that produce perfectionism and other methods employed to deny and cover up one's true state. A person who feels ashamed is inhibited in his ability to love God and to develop healthy relationships.

6) Emotional numbness. This state is usually a symptom of unresolved and hidden anger. The person who overanticipates being disappointed shields himself by shutting off his positive and negative emotional reactions. This affects his ability to sense God's presence, to worship Him, even to enjoy living. It renders him capable of insensitive, hurtful actions toward others, and produces a continual desire for sensational, emotional experiences. The emotionally numb person will usually gravitate toward crises or even create or escalate crises to some degree—something to stimulate his numb emotions and validate his reason for living. It is hard for crisis-oriented Christians with numb emotions to "lie down in green pastures" and chew the cud. They always have to be active.

7) Compulsive-addictive behavior. Many of the indulgent sins of the flesh such as immorality, gluttony, drunkenness, greed proceed out of addictive behavioral patterns. A Christian may have the Source of healing resident within him, but when his mind is not renewed, all efforts to resist temptation fail. He is driven repeatedly into the addictive cycle, repeating his compulsions and feeling guilty each time. Many substance abusers substitute more acceptable addictions, such as food or work, in place of drug and alcohol addiction when they come to Christ. While they once slaved for the devil, now they slave for the

Lord, driven to be active and justifying this behavior as godly.

8) Anger. The most often denied emotion in the Body of Christ is anger. In many circles, it is considered sinful. Gulping down this emotion in order to look more spiritual is directly responsible for emotional numbness and depression, which are, next to marriage problems, the major counseling issues dealt with in the pastor's study. Hidden anger is actually the root of bitterness talked about by the writer of Hebrews.

But what do these eight emotional wounds do to a Christian? My experience has shown that they produce the following six results in Christians' lives:

1) A distorted view of God and the inability to feel the joy of His presence.

2) The lack of joyful motivation to pray or receive comfort from prayer.

3) The inability to know and carry out the will of God for one's life.

4) The impaired ability to understand the Bible and receive comfort from its words.

5) The redefining of the first priority of the Christian life as usefulness, service and ministry rather than worshiping and loving God.

6) The inability to make long-lasting commitments to the church, in marriage and with friendships.

I don't know a single true Christian who is not anxious to be used by God, but very often the wounded soul postpones the period of greatest usefulness to Him. God is not a user and abuser of people. He doesn't call people to serve until they are first worshipers. The disciples loved and followed Jesus, sitting at His feet before they were ever sent out. Mary was exonerated by the Lord when criticized by her sister, Martha, for not prioritizing service over spiritual growth. The Lord will first restore to health, helping the Christian find the joy of God's presence before He leads him into service. Bringing forth fruit is a byproduct of living in Christ, not a separate duty.

A Lesson from Leviticus

Many believers eschew studying Leviticus, but its clear patterns speak loud messages to Christians. Believe it or not, Leviticus has a wonderful message to the wounded soul.

Before the New Covenant period of grace, available to us because of Jesus Christ, the Law of Moses reigned and God's nature was veiled in its thousands of laws and rigid regulations. One of these passages seems at first harsh until you understand the reason for it. In the twenty-first chapter is a list of the physical qualifications for an Old Covenant priest.

> Then the Lord spoke to Moses, saying, . . . "No man of your offspring throughout their generations who has a defect shall approach to offer the bread of his God. For no one who has a defect shall approach: a blind man, or a lame man, or he who has a disfigured face, or any deformed limb, or a man who has a broken foot or broken hand, or a hunchback or a dwarf, or one who has a defect in his eye or eczema or scabs or crushed testicles. No man among the descendants of Aaron the priest, who has a defect, is to come near to offer the Lord's offerings. . . . He may eat the bread of his God, both of the most holy and of the holy, only he shall not go in to the veil or come near the altar because he has a defect, that he may not profane My sanctuaries." Leviticus 21:16–20

What are we seeing? Is God so cruel as to hinder the maimed and lame from coming to Him and being used? Before you think that God is the ultimate in perfectionistic expectations, look a little closer. God did not want His reputation to be established as one who extracted some of the most difficult and backbreaking work in Israel, the duties of priesthood, from those who had had the misfortune to be born deformed or who had been afflicted with diseases.

How could a blind man see to light the lampstand? How could a wounded man help lift a thousand-pound bull to the altar of sacrifice? How could a God who is good expect a man in physical pain to work from dawn till dusk in the heat of the desert or stand in the house of God by night? How could the Author of life expect a man living with the disappointment of being unable to conceive life bless the children and circumcise the sons of other men?

The same God who later said, "The sabbath was made for man, not man for the sabbath," also wrote these qualifications into the job description of His priests. In order to serve God without a sense of failure, a priest would have to be physically able. If he were sick, he would have to be healed first before he could serve. Until that day, he could nourish himself on the privileges of priesthood—eating the choicest meats and sweet-smelling breads, being provided for financially, unlike the maimed in other tribes. His lot in life was eased by the goodness of God because of being Aaron's son. He enjoyed the "perks" with none of the works!

Can you see the parallel for the child of God? When you join His family, His first priority in your life is to restore you to health, to heal you of the wounds you suffered while laboring under dysfunctional traditions and trying to work your way back to Him. He wants you to see before you have to lead the blind. He wants His power in your hands before you try the impossible. He wants you to grow into the full stature of Christ before you have to shoulder the weight of His responsibilities. Jesus wants you nurtured, soothed and healed before you serve.

He Restores My Soul

How does healing take place? What part do I play and what does God want me to do? When you read the Bible with the legalistic veil removed, Jesus is clearly seen as the Good Shepherd, the healer of wounds and the restorer of souls. In fact, the Hebrew word for *restore* means "to return, to give back." The word *soul* in Hebrew means "the mind and emotions." Correctly translated, "He restoreth my soul" actually means "He gives my emotions back." It is not beyond the power of God to take anyone regardless of the dysfunctions of his life and heal him of his wounds, restoring his emotions to full function. Jesus laid down His own life and in so doing redeemed mankind from the curse of the Law. He suffered so that the destructive effects of the curse need not find their full vent on His sheep.

Whereas Adam failed, Jesus Christ made it through. Adam sinned; Jesus did not. Adam sweat; Jesus sweat great drops of blood. If Adam suffered separation and the feelings of rejection, Jesus Christ suffered more, experiencing total abandonment. Adam lost his position; Jesus willingly relinquished His, giving up His heavenly glory, His reputation. He bore the full pain and sorrow of the mistakes of Adam and his sons, tasting death for every person. And in place of our powerlessness, He sent the Holy Spirit, the fountain of renewal, so that our souls could be restored.

We are well-fed spiritually, anointed joyfully with His oil of gladness, protected, loved and secure—transformed into a magnificent specimen of what a "healthy" sheep should be.

There is no such thing as an emotionally restored soul that does not know Jesus Christ. In some way each lost sheep is outside the pasture gazing longingly at the greener grass inside.

The soul that is lost has only to call out to the Good Shepherd for help and the pasture's gate will swing open for him. If you are reading this and know you are outside His fold or that you need His restorative touch, why not stop now and ask the Good Shepherd to become your Shepherd? You might pray this prayer: "Lord Jesus, I am like the dog who was abused or a sheep who is lost. I open the gate of my heart and life to You and ask You to become my Shepherd, my Lord and Savior. Amen."

Praying that prayer is the first step in seeing your wounded soul restored.

Although no one is completely healthy emotionally without Jesus Christ, there are many Christians who settle for life at the edge of the pasture. They do not follow the Lord closely and do not hear His soothing voice as clearly as others do. Those who follow afar off are in danger of being bushwhacked by the predator. They are seldom anointed with oil and burn out grazing under the hot sun. They are prone to wander farther away from God the Father, without clear direction for the paths of righteousness.

It is only the Good Shepherd who can lead the sheep back into a relationship with the Father. Staying close to Jesus Christ is the first key to having the soul restored. Not only does the wounded sheep need to call out to the Good Shepherd, but a commitment to follow Jesus more closely will position him for restoration.

But why do some sheep after meeting Jesus Christ seem to stay as far away from Him as possible? Why don't His healing words soothe their souls? Let's look in the next chapter at an all-important aspect adult children must consider.

8
Healing the Child Within

Children receive four things from their fathers: approval, affection, protection and provision. If they do not find them in their own fathers, they spend the rest of their lives looking for them.

Actress Sophia Loren was abandoned by her father when she was a little girl. She and her sister, Maria, were the daughters he had had by his mistress. They were never given his name and grew up in poverty in a small village in Italy near Naples. As I read about her story in *Parade* magazine (January 31, 1988), I was touched by her comments.

"It was the dream of my life to have a father, and that is why I sought him everywhere. I spent much of my life looking for substitutes for him." Sophia's marriage to Carlo Ponti, a man seventeen years her senior, is one evidence that in her relationships with men, she is still looking for her father. Sophia saw her father only six times in her life and yet she says, "He shaped my life more than any other man." After her fa-

103

ther became terminally ill, Sophia learned that he had spent hours alone in theaters watching her films. Clutching at the single, tiny remnant of her relationship with him, she says, "With all the grandiose gifts I have received in my life, my greatest possession is the only toy my father ever gave me, a little blue auto with my name on it."

Sophia Loren's sadness is shared by millions of children the world over. More than twelve million American children live in fatherless homes at any given moment and an even higher percentage are fatherless for a significant part of their childhoods. One British study of the population of women's prisons found that more than a third of the prisoners were fatherless (see *Like Father, Like Daughter* by Suzanne Fields, p. 63). Even these large figures do not reflect the emotional pain of the millions whose fathers died or who are victims of their father's physical or sexual abuse, neglect, harsh words or cold silence, as was the case with Ann Feldman.

Growing Up without Affection

Ann Feldman's father is a Holocaust survivor who saw his mother and sister die of starvation at Dachau in spite of all his efforts to smuggle food to them. Bernie Hirsch's nightmare included stays at two other concentration camps before the Allies liberated them in 1944. In order to stay alive, Bernie worked harder than the rest and was rewarded with favors from the guards, extra gloves and pants to shield his body from the acid in the Nazi munitions factory where he worked.

After the war, Bernie visited Israel and met Ann's mother, Miriam, whom he married after knowing her only a week. The marriage was the product of a Jewish matchmaker. Miriam's mother had been unable to care for her and had left her at an orphanage in Israel where their only meals were often bread smeared with shortening. At only seven years old, she worked eight-hour days ironing the clothes in the laundry of the institution. Miriam was eager to marry and escape the pain of her childhood, but she didn't know how hard it would be to live with a man who had survived the hellish horrors of three Nazi concentration camps.

Bernie almost never spoke, never initiated conversation, as though his mind was preoccupied with reliving his macabre victimization. He seethed in a silent world of anger that found no vent except compulsive self-deprivation.

Emotionally, Bernie was still living at Dachau even after he moved to the United States. There was little money, but it didn't matter because Bernie had survived for four years of the war wearing tattered clothing, eating meager rations and drinking polluted water in the unheated barracks of the camps.

Ann was born into this family of survivors and grew up inheriting a legacy of deprivation. Her father saved everything. One meal would be made to last for days, her father eating food that was spoiled rather than throw it out. He was insensitive to ordinary needs of growing girls, and Ann's mother had to plead with him to furnish her clothing. "*Nedafnesh!*" he would flare in Yiddish. "Not necessary!"

Ann grew up abandoned emotionally by her father. She reared herself because her mother was drifting into her own independent world, working full-time to buy any extras for herself and Ann. Her parents didn't know how to love because they had never been taught. They never showed each other or Ann affection. Ann never remembers her father initiating a conversation with her, taking her anywhere or hugging her. "There were times," recalls Ann, "when I felt love for my daddy so much that I would run up to him, grab him and hug him, but he would pull away as though he were afraid to hug me." He often worked eighteen hours a day hiding from his family. When it came time to give money to Ann, in her words it was as if "he and his money were one, and that giving it away was like giving away pieces of himself."

Children who grow up without proper parenting are robbed of love and nurturing, important ingredients in emotional development. When the parents do not provide the basic needs children grow up starved emotionally. Ann's life still bears the scars of her father's emotional abandonment—instead of approval she was ignored; instead of affection she was never touched; instead of protection she was undisciplined and left to raise and train herself; and instead of provision she learned the life of a survivor, deprived of things children normally have. She felt ashamed and that her home was "different," a feeling that has permeated her life and affected her self-esteem.

Had Ann's father tried, he could not have done a better job of passing on dysfunction to his daughter. But the truth is, Ann does not have to continue limping through life. As the apostle Peter wrote, "You were called for this very purpose, that you might inherit a blessing." It is to the deep cavity of emotional deprivation that God sends the essence of the Gospel—to the hurting child within.

The Child Within

The term *adult children* is not original with me, but is born out of a growing movement of people who are beginning to realize that they are lacking in some aspect of emotional maturity as a result of growing up in dysfunctional homes.

Children of alcoholics, like Glenn in chapter 5, who have to assume the responsibilities of surrogate husbands and fathers, experience things that no child should have to—or no adult, for that matter. Retrieving his father from the bar and being the "crutch" for his family robbed Glenn of the privilege of being a child and developing gradually through stages of maturity. Children who at age six must get up and fix their own breakfasts because Mother is too drunk, or children who are used as pawns in parental arguments, miss out on childhood.

Janet Geringer Woititz, author of *Adult Children of Alcoholics*, lists in her book thirteen characteristics that set this group of people apart from others. They are as follows:

"Adult Children of Alcoholics

1) guess at what normal behavior is.

2) have difficulty following a project through from beginning to end.

3) lie when it would be just as easy to tell the truth.

4) judge themselves without mercy.

5) have difficulty having fun.

6) take themselves very seriously.

7) have difficulty with intimate relationships.

8) overreact to changes over which they have no control.

9) constantly seek approval and affirmation.

10) usually feel that they are different from other people.

11) are super responsible or super irresponsible.

12) are extremely loyal, even in the face of evidence that the loyalty is undeserved.

13) are impulsive, locking themselves into a course of action without giving serious consideration to alternative behaviors or possible consequences. This impulsivity leads to confusion, self-

loathing, and loss of control over their environment. In addition, they spend an excessive amount of energy cleaning up the mess."

Recognizing Childishness

As you will probably agree, many of these characteristics are evidences of emotional immaturity and childishness. It is as though their emotional development was stymied. Because of this, adult children move through life physically developed as adults, but childish in their emotional reactions. Let's examine some of the qualities of children and how they apply to emotionally stymied adults.

1) Self-Centeredness

From the time a baby is born he is usually centered on himself. He knows only that he wants something and that he wants it now. This could be anything: a diaper change, his next meal or a toy he spies while riding in the grocery cart. He does not understand or care about what the needs of other people in his environment might be; his needs are his only consideration. He cannot postpone the fulfillment of his need or desire because he has no concept of time.

I have often noticed an abrasive insistence among children from dysfunctional homes. It is as though they cannot postpone the fulfillment of needs for fear that they may never be met. This is easier to understand when you realize that their parents often promised things to them, but never delivered. "I'll get you a new bike"—and it was forgotten. "I'll be at your graduation"—and he was drunk in a bar.

But now that the adult child has grown up and is dealing with others, many of whom are emotionally mature, his insistence on his own way breeds conflict and rejection.

2) Immature Understanding of Responsibility

Children are notably deficient in understanding the importance of fulfilling certain responsibilities. They are extremely compulsive, vacillating between thoughts and ideas often within a few seconds. Their attention spans are short, keeping them moving from one interest to the next in a flurry of activity.

This childish characteristic is seen in the adult child's inability to follow projects through from beginning to end. Other adult children overcompensate for their fears, pushing and shoving themselves to the bitter end, often flogging a dead horse.

3) Fantasizing

It is normal for a child to dream and to develop a vivid imagination. Many of the dreams he dreams as a child influence the development of goals for his life's work. Walt Disney came from a very rigid home where his father was strict, exacting and verbally abusive. He dreamed dreams that have come to pass and provided joy for millions.

But what happens if none of your childhood dreams comes to pass? The tendency is to live life in a fantasy world. The soaring market for romance novels is one evidence that emotionally deprived women are still waiting to be rescued from their boredom by Prince Charming. When life does not measure up to the fantasies, the adult child continues to look for the fulfillment of his dreams in relationships and experiences. When they are disappointing, he drops those toys and looks for another place where life is magical and perfect, idolizing people and places as settings for his "novels." His fantasizing drastically affects his ability to know what normal is and keeps him from developing intimate relationships in which acceptance of certain faults is foundational for success.

4) Tantrums

A child knows only one way of making his needs and wishes known, particularly if the fulfillment is not forthcoming within his short attention span. Crying, hitting other playmates, snatching things for himself are his first options. But if those strategies don't work, he escalates the battle. He holds his breath until he turns blue, throws himself down kicking and screaming or takes his toys and goes home.

My friend Janet Laughlin holds a master's degree in child development and works at a school for underprivileged children. She shared with me how one little girl named Tamika kept running away from the group and hiding in the schoolyard. Try as they might, they could not make her stand still and learn.

The principal decided on a new ploy. Whenever Tamika ran away, instead of scolding her, they ran after her, teasing her as if she were playing a game. They discovered that she craved attention. She wanted to know if anyone cared enough about her to run after her. In the past, she had received negative reinforcement when she ran away, which satisfied her craving until her next opportunity. But when the teachers began to make a game out of it, she gradually stopped.

Adult children do the same things. Some are excellent manipulators with tears, some are verbally and physically abusive. Some adopt less overt strategies—withholding love and approval until their desires are met. The miffed spouse stomps up to his room and slams the door or, worse, packs his bags and leaves. His actions are reactionary, irrational and childish. This is not to say that all expressions of anger are childish. Anger is a valid emotion and as we will see in another chapter needs to find its proper vent. But tactics like these only escalate rather than resolve. If their manipulative tactics do not work, adult children often cannot stand the humiliation and abandon commitments and people.

5) Cruelty

It's hard to picture when you are gazing at little "dolls" nestled in their beds in an aura of innocence that only a few hours before they were slapping each other and calling each other names. It is within the child's ability to say both the kindest and cruelest things—on purpose. Children are insensitive to the ways their words and actions affect others. And when they are told they usually don't care because of their self-centeredness. This abrasiveness can continue through adulthood. The verbal abuser, in fact, has never grown up and matured in his ability to express his own emotions without injuring others. It is seen in those who do not know how to be anything but blunt in their conversations and observations.

Other adult children store up what they would like to say and spill it all out at the wrong time or in awkward circumstances, embarrassing themselves and others. Inappropriate crying, nervous laughter, making one's friends and loved ones the brunt of sarcastic jokes all demonstrate the insensitivity that is characteristic of many adult children.

Balancing the Good

There are other characteristics of children—good ones—that have the capacity to get adult children into trouble simply because they do not know the appropriate limits of these behaviors. Let's look at how these appear in the lives of adult children.

1) Pleasing Others

A child's need for approval and affirmation is great. Withholding it can be cruel and cause permanent emotional damaging. Children are naturally eager to please unless something has happened to shatter their world and make them cynical.

My mother taught school for forty years. The first fifteen were in elementary school and the last 25 in high school. She found marked differences in the age groups with respect to responding to questions. In her fourth-grade classes, children strained to get their hands high enough, turning them into wiggling flags to get her attention. But the high school students were a different matter. A few would raise their hands matter-of-factly, as though embarrassed still to be eager to answer questions. The desire to receive approval from authority figures seemed to have been transferred to receiving appproval from their peers. But in each teenager was still the desire to hear an encouraging word from the teacher.

Likewise, adult children characteristically have insatiable appetites for validation, as though their approval cavern is bottomless. They thrive on it, looking for it everywhere. In our church, after each service, adult children sometimes crowd around us at the altar wanting to share their spiritual experiences and insights and looking to have the decisions they have made appreciated and validated. What they want is what they have never heard: "Mommy is so proud of you! You are the best child in the United States!"

In order to attempt to fill this cavern with approval, they become pleasers on the job, at church, at the P.T.A. and in the home. Any unprincipled people who discovered this could manipulate these adult children, laying guilt trips on them and extracting anything from them—money, time, loyalty, sacrifice. It is this childish tendency that causes them to become codependent, hooked on solving problems and rescuing unfortunates, working themselves to death to please authority figures.

2) Desire for Stability

It is hard to live in a state of unpredictability. I have noticed how much calmer and happier young children seem to be whose mothers try hard to enforce some structure in the home—eating meals at approximately the same times, keeping the house clean, getting them to bed at the same time and spending quality time with them each day. This can be overdone, of course, but from what I have seen, it is all too rare.

Children who grew up in dysfunctional homes, unless they were compulsively rigid, often had no stability. Life was completely unpredictable. The schedule was either nonexistent, because the parents were too preoccupied to care about the home, or frequently disrupted by the compulsive-abusive behavior of the problem person. One of the things adult children long for is peace that comes, they believe, from stability they never had as children.

This desire for stability can easily become a fear of instability. When circumstances or conditions change, adult children sometimes feel betrayed. Once again they feel flung into an unpredictable situation over which they have no control. They begin to overreact, either assigning a higher degree of importance to the change or stubbornly refusing to give in to it.

I have pitied some pastors who had to relocate their church buildings. Most churches are full of adult children who think of all sorts of "spiritual" reasons why changes in location cannot be the will of God. They will cite the amount of money being spent or the fact that the leaders didn't pray about it long enough. While these objections are true in some cases, more often than not the fear of change is at work. Adult children will sometimes stir strife and opposition rather than move into a new—and therefore insecure—dimension. This applies to new dimensions of spiritual maturity as well.

3) The Ability to Have Fun

Normal children grow up with plenty of time to play. In healthy homes, parents read to their children, play games with them, take them to the park and enter into their fun and excitement.

But children from dysfunctional homes are subconsciously preoccupied with tragedies beyond their control—alcoholism, a handicap, poverty, the breakup of their parents' marriage. It is as though they can never get away from it or get it off their minds completely. When parents are absorbed in their own pain as well, children grow up not knowing how to have fun or needing permission from someone somewhere to go out and enjoy life. Survivors of the Great Depression sometimes have difficulty letting themselves go for fear that it all will be wiped away, the dream will shatter. Some even believe that having fun is wrong.

Adult children behave in the same way. They don't know how to have fun and when they do, they often feel guilty about it. Taking children to Disney World can be a chore, but fun is healing to the emotions and a form of rest to the body. And let's face it, if you don't have a body, you don't have a ministry. And if your soul hurts, you can't enjoy God.

In order to be healed, the adult child must start having fun little by little, treating himself to small doses of good, clean pleasure. If you feel identification here you need to retrain your overdeveloped sense of guilt. Learn to react to things that are sinful rather than things that are just plain fun—like buying a new dress or going to a baseball game. It is possible, of course, to become a lover of pleasure, but this is not your problem. Let your budget have an item for fun and relaxation. And all the workaholics reading this need to take a vacation—and leave your briefcases at home! It will take trial and error before you achieve balance, but that is how you learn.

These qualities are manifestations of a deprived childhood, characteristic of all adult children. Unless the pain from the past is addressed, the wounds that foster these qualities will never be healed. But healing is possible. We can reach the wounded child within and help him develop into a healthy, mature child of God. This begins when the adult child submits his life to God.

Healing the Child Within

It is more than coincidence that the scriptural metaphors describing salvation are in terms of birth and parenting. Each soul who comes to Jesus Christ for redemption is a hurting "child" who has missed a crucial aspect of parenting; regardless of how great anyone's father was, he failed in some aspect. Even parenting at its best cannot meet our deepest needs. Unless our heavenly Father breathes into our nostrils a second breath, the breath of spiritual life, we will be eternally lost; the fear of abandonment will find its horrible prophetic fulfillment.

But how does this happen? Nicodemus, a Pharisee who came one night to see Jesus, asked the same question. Frustrated because he couldn't understand the spiritual metaphor Jesus used—*born again*—he asked, "How can a man be born when he is old? He cannot enter a second time into his mother's womb and be born, can he?" What adult children want is what Jesus promised: a new chance to live, free from the binding effects of parents who failed, who by their actions and inactions, willful or accidental, wounded us within. To be born again conjures up pictures of childlike vulnerability and innocence, as though one could have a fresh start, free and clear, and, as far as God is concerned, with no previous existence, no marred and scarred past.

What God wants most is to become your parent, whether or not you came from a dysfunctional home. He wants to take responsibility for your welfare to provide approval, affection, protection and provision. He brings to the relationship not a childish, dysfunctional being, but an almighty, perfect, loving and gracious Father who is able to restore you to health, to blot out your sins, the times you have "missed the mark," and adopt you as His own. If this sounds like a dream, it isn't. God is waiting for your response to His offer.

Jesus explained it one day to His disciples. He called a small child to come and stand in the middle of them and then said, "Unless you are converted and become like children, you shall not enter the kingdom of heaven. Whoever then humbles himself as this child, he is the greatest in the kingdom of heaven" (Matthew 18:3–4). The burly, worldly-wise disciples were amazed. How could being childlike help a person respond to God?

If God wants to be your Father, to adopt you as one of His own, to nurture you, give you a new name and take responsibility for you, He wants you to become like a child. We have seen childlike qualities—"bad" ones that the adult child may copy, and "good" ones that he may not be able to copy. Let's examine now the qualities of childlikeness that God is looking for in those who want to become His children or grow in a greater knowledge of His Fatherhood.

1) Powerlessness

Self-sufficiency is a manifestation of fear and pride. It makes us isolated and independent, deluded into thinking that we can save ourselves with our human powers and maintain that salvation by our own efforts. Rather, we need to "shrink" in powerlessness before almighty God.

I am not speaking here of low self-esteem or unworthiness, but in terms of strength. Children realize their limitations and rely on their fathers to provide the muscle power they themselves lack. "My daddy can do anything!" is the usual verbalization of a child's perception of his strength—and a statement of his own weakness in relation to it. Beginning to view yourself as powerless causes you to become aware of how dependent you are upon God and how much you expect Him to do.

2) Vulnerability

To become powerless is to lower your defenses and become vulnerable to God. Walls of defensiveness keep you far from a revelation of the Fatherhood of God because your emotions wall Him out. Children are vulnerable and need protection.

I will never forget the times I lay in the hospital, a new mother, holding each of my babies. How much they needed protecting! They were totally defenseless. Their lives depended on my character, my assuming the responsibility to care for them. I felt overwhelmed with the desire to hold them in my arms and felt a twinge of sadness knowing that they would experience hurts and pain someday. It made me determined to let nothing harm them if I could possibly help it. Vulnerability draws the compassion of the Almighty in the same way.

3) Innocence

Small children do not and should not know very much about evil. They will learn soon enough through the hard knocks of life. Children who become streetwise lose trust and become cynical. Adults who believe that God does not have their best interests at heart have fallen prey to the serpent's lie in the Garden of Eden and have hardened their hearts. To believe that God is watching out for you, that you do not have to be hyper-vigilant and aware of evils that may befall you, is the highest expression of faith. Leaving the analysis to God is one way to return to innocence. Another way is to stop indulging in evil as though that world does not even exist. Paul wrote to the church at Corinth: "In evil be babes . . . " (1 Corinthians 14:20).

4) Ingenuousness

Children possess a naïveté that is refreshing. Ingenuousness in adults might come across to the worldly-wise as stupidity or needless vulnerability, but have you noticed how the truly ingenuous possess deep inner peace? They know the benefits of trust—an inner happiness that the world can never achieve for all its striving.

My son, Billy, is eleven years old and still possesses this ingenuousness that makes life fresh. He assumes that everyone has the same motive he has for doing things. He also takes it upon himself to explain life to me at times, disbelieving that others have selfish ambitions and intentions. This quality of childlikeness is what Paul meant in 1 Corinthians 13 when he wrote that love "bears all things, believes all things, hopes all things, endures all things" (verse 7).

5) Trust

Because children are ingenuous, they possess an honest faith in the goodness of adults even when it isn't there. Only repeated betrayal of this faith wears it down, as has happened to adult children. But in order to experience the Fatherhood of God, the adult must become childlike once again in his willingness to trust. This time, instead of placing his trust in fallible people, it is time to place trust in God and leave it there.

The author of Hebrews wrote: "This hope we have as an anchor of the soul, both sure and steadfast, that enters within the veil [the presence of God]." The anchors of ancient ships were not dropped to the bottom of the sea like those of modern times. The anchor was lowered into a boat and sailors rowed to shore and flung the anchor between two strong crossbars that formed a "V." It hung there, tethering the ship safely in the harbor. In order to approach the shore, the sailors reeled the ship in on its own anchor. As tides ebbed and flowed or storms arose, the anchor remained in the "V," held steadfast to the shore. The childlike faith that God wants in each of us is the faith that anchors in Him, always believing that regardless of circumstances He has hold of us.

6) Hope

Children also possess a marvelous ability to hope. They have the opposite of a sour, pessimistic attitude that is common to so many survivors—the thought that things will get worse instead of better, that there is no hope, that God will not help me or hear me. At its heart this is cynicism. Healthy children believe that life will get better, that there will be a day in which they can live happy lives. To this end they dream and prepare.

To destroy hope is to put a stumblingblock in front of a child. Jesus promised that those who caused one of His little ones to stumble would one day wish that a heavy millstone were hung around their necks and that they were drowned in the sea rather than face God's righteous anger. This is how precious our hope in God, the Almighty, is to Him. He protects it with a vengeance.

7) Teachability

Children are willing to be taught. Their eagerness to learn, to prove they can accomplish and please, is refreshing. They will readily admit that they do not know everything and need someone to take them by the hand and lead them. They love it, in fact, when adults spend time with them, patiently showing them how. God wants this quality in all of us, the absence of shame about what we don't know and the hunger to find out all we can about Him and the environment in which He has placed us. This teachable quality is an evidence of true humility.

Simon Peter, for all his rough edges, was truly teachable. His spiritual maturity level was never concealed because he blurted out his innermost thoughts to Jesus and everyone else. But he learned how to act and behave and what was right and wrong from the Master Teacher Himself.

Adult children have difficulty remaining teachable because of their lack of trust, but adopting the view of yourself as a learner rather than a teacher or an authority endears you to others and prevents pride from gaining a foothold in your life. A missionary friend of ours was told by one of his Bible college professors, "Son, be a learner a long time." Why not always? Even the greatest teachers remain great because of their ability to keep learning.

8) Wonder

Because of their teachable qualities, little children are filled with wonder. They love to learn new things about their environment and are fascinated by how things work. They are visibly moved by things we take for granted—shapes of clouds, flowers poking up out of the ground, insects molting and water boiling. God put us in His creation to enjoy and admire it.

My close friend Roberta Crane is a grandmother and pastor of a large church in Kansas City. I was with her the first time she saw the Grand Canyon. She gasped, cried and started singing to the Lord about how marvelous He is to have made such a thing! Her response was genuine wonder. This is the substance of real worship, not form and ritual. How God feels at this type of response is akin to the feeling a parent has when little children squeal happily over the Christmas gifts we give them. The things God has created for our joy, the blessings He shares with us and even the valuable lessons we have learned in times of heartache need to move us visibly to a sincere, worshipful awe of God who is truly almighty.

Adopting These Qualities

Each of these childlike qualities can be adopted by hardened, so-called wise adults who want to experience the joy of God's presence. Many Christians have lost their sense of God's approval, affection, protection and provision because they are trying to bypass stages of maturity and act like know-it-alls.

Becoming like a child is difficult for adult children who want to be in control, who are perfectionistic and rigid. In order to do it, you have to give up control and see yourself as God does, the helpless little child He has always longed to adopt. Taking on these eight qualities we have just discussed draws you to the presence of God like metal shavings to a magnet. Make them a matter of prayer and earnest desire. Here's how.

1) Retreat into Childlikeness

Stress is the order of the day for adults who have to care for themselves and others. When the pressure becomes too great, retreat into childlikeness. Learn how to shrink in size from the spiritual giant you think you have to be and become a little child again, even if it's only for a little while.

I remember going through a stage of religious perfectionism in which I fasted and prayed overzealously for revival. If anyone was going to see revival, I was. I became morose and intense, believing that God expected some level of spiritual performance beyond my capacity to deliver. During this time, I became ill with severe stomach pains. They lasted for hours. As I cried out to God for relief, I broke down and started to cry like a baby. I still remember the sense of God's presence I felt immediately. All my religious fervor could not work up the closeness to Him that one instant of childlikeness brought. God started working in my life to break off the religious facade I had placed around myself. He showed me He couldn't reward all my fervor because it was a mask I had made to cover up the perception I had of myself as someone flawed, defective and disapproved of by God. But when I began to shrink before God, He came running to meet me—the real me! It was then I could really talk to God. As my ability to let go increased, my stomach pains disappeared and have not returned since.

2) Pray Like a Child

This means talking to God as if you were a child, expressing yourself simply, the way a small child would talk to her daddy. When you talk to God without pretension, you drop your facade and make yourself vulnerable to Him. Great vibrato and religious phraseology never give you the sense of having touched God at the deepest level. Why not start talking to God as if you trust Him to understand and care? You will be amazed to sense how close God is to you. It is O.K. to tell God you don't understand everything and that you are tired of trying to figure everything out. You need to be hugged and nurtured and you are coming to Him with your arms outstretched.

3) Worship at a Childlike Level

Sandra Simpson LeSourd, author of *The Compulsive Woman*, was a guest speaker at our church's women's retreat two years ago. She taught us about issues facing those who are afflicted with addictions and compulsions. During one session we decided to spend time in worship with the songs we had learned as children in Sunday school—"My Best Friend Is Jesus," "Jesus Loves Me," "Jesus Loves the Little Children" and "This Little Light of Mine." After we were finished, teary mascara was running down many faces. Many women were visibly moved as the ministry penetrated a deeper level. Everyone went away feeling edified and sensing God's presence. Why? We all came to God as little children who needed a Father's love. We had truly retreated into childlikeness and found our Father waiting.

4) Admiring the Child You Were

One of my friends is the grandchild, child, wife and mother of alcoholics. She has never known a time without active alcoholism. Recovering from the shame and the pain it brings has not been easy, and she has wisely sought professional counseling.

She has always had problems liking herself and was amazed when the counselor offered this advice. He told her to find a picture of herself as a little girl, put it in a prominent place and compliment the picture whenever she passed by it, saying things like, "You sure are a doll!" "I love you to pieces!" "You are so cute!" These were things she never heard as a child. Within a few weeks, she began to see drastic improvement in her attitude toward herself. She began to love herself in a healthy way rather than remain dissatisfied with the way God made her. "I can honestly say today that I like myself just the way I am," she told me recently.

5) Read Children's Bible Stories

Another way to retreat into childlikeness is reading children's Bible stories. Children's literature is loaded with the gospel of grace, majoring on the theme of God's unconditional love. Why do we change the message for the more "mature"? During my period of intense religious fervor, reading to my children always brought a respite from the cold, hard "gospel" of perfectionistic works that I was preaching unknowingly. Tears would often well up in my eyes as I read simple phrases that crystallized the essence of God's love, lines like "Peter started looking at the waves; and he stopped looking at Jesus" or "The shepherd had many lambs and sheep in His flock; one little lamb strayed away and got lost. . . . You are Jesus' little lamb. He loves you and will always watch over you."

Why not pick out a few children's books, ones with lifelike illustrations, and read them each night before you go to bed? You will be amazed at the sharp clarity of revelation of God's love and the soothing balm it will bring to your works-oriented soul that is trying too hard to feel loved by God.

These suggestions work, regardless of your maturity level. This is because childlikeness is the key to establishing a relationship with God as well as maintaining fellowship with Him. That is how Ann Feldman, the Jewish daughter of the Holocaust survivor, found Jesus Christ.

Ironically, it was her parents' failure that brought her to the Lord. Her parents' preoccupation with their own lives and their inability to care for her meant she was often dropped off at the homes of babysitters. It was in the home of a babysitter that Ann first heard about Jesus.

As she drifted off to sleep in the room of the babysitter's daughter, she saw a crucifix on the wall. Not knowing who it was, she asked the little girl in the bed next to her.

"That's Jesus," exclaimed the little girl. "He's dying for our sins. Do you believe in Jesus?"

And Ann remembers replying, "Shhh. Don't tell anybody. But I believe Jesus died for my sins, too."

At age sixteen, after an emotionally agonizing childhood, Ann committed herself publicly to Jesus Christ at the messianic Jewish center in the city where she lived. That night as she prayed, her mind drifted back to that night when, at age five, abandoned emotionally by her parents, the Lord Jesus Christ had taken her up, put His hand on her life and guided her footsteps until she could find Him again.

The secret, then, of healing the child within is finding God as the loving, faithful, promise-keeping Parent who can be trusted implicitly with your childlike faith. Now let us move on and experience another key to His healing grace, the removal of shame.

9
Taking the Sting Out of Shame

Before we begin our study of shame, take a pencil and answer *yes* or *no* to the following questions:

_____ 1. Is there some memory of your past that makes you cringe or afraid it will be discovered?

_____ 2. Do you feel "different" from others?

_____ 3. Do you believe that if others knew your secret, they might react in a way that would hurt you emotionally?

_____ 4. Do you have the underlying feeling that you are inferior to others?

_____ 5. Do you work hard to try to improve your performance so others will respect you and admire your work?

_____ 6. Do you feel that you would like to achieve more to be respected?

_____ 7. Do you find yourself projecting an image to others that is different from the way your family knows you or you know yourself to be?

_____ 8. Do you find yourself taking on the mannerisms and speech habits of those you admire?

_____ 9. Are you envious of others' advantages?

_____ 10. Are you ashamed to show emotions and to "feel" feelings that are natural?

_____ 11. If married: Do you feel inhibited sexually toward your spouse?

_____ 12. Do you have trouble admitting your own weaknesses and shortcomings to yourself and others?

_____ 13. Are you shy around those you should by now feel comfortable with?

_____ 14. Are you embarrassed at all about the family you came from or your present station in life?

_____ 15. Do you starve or tranquilize how you truly feel about yourself with compulsive behaviors such as shopping, work, sex, gambling or addictions to food, nicotine, caffeine, drugs or alcohol?

_____ 16. Are you dissatisfied with any aspect of your personality or appearance?

_____ 17. Are you feeling compelled to minimize the questions on this test as irrelevant to the diagnosing of true shame?

_____ 18. Do you feel that people should quit talking about all this nonsense, forget it and go on with life?

_____ 19. Do you feel nervous or afraid to talk about certain aspects of your past or present?

_____ 20. Do memories of childhood experiences bring you pain or embarrassment when you think of them?

Score: People who are ashamed when they should not be will likely answer yes to any of the questions above. I would estimate that if you gave more than four yes answers you are affected, if you gave more than eight you are very shame-based, and if you gave more than twelve you are extremely shame-based. Let's read on to begin to deal with the shame in our lives.

Recognizing Shame

When Karen was growing up in Pittsburgh during World War II, there was minimal public awareness about alcoholism. As far as she can remember, her mother never said the word *alcoholic* in reference to her father who drank six days a week and was never home. In fact, Karen's mother never said one unkind word about her father, bolstering his image to the children by praising him for being a hard worker. But Karen and her three brothers and one sister watched silently as alcoholism destroyed their father's life and left a cruel legacy for the next generation—claiming Karen's brother who also became an alcoholic and committed suicide.

All the roles typical to alcoholic families were present in Karen's home. Her sister was the caretaker, helping her mother clean, cook and sew for the family. Her brother was the hero, always excelling in school. Karen was the lost child living in a fantasy world. One particular memory lines the walls of her mind with the constant gloom of shame, the feeling of being different.

Every Saturday, she and the other children would board the city bus and ride to the show. Her father always insisted on going, and he was always drunk. And when he was drunk he became hostile, starting arguments, swearing. Heads would turn to look.

Karen relayed the biting memory to me: "I used to sit as far in the front of the bus as possible, hoping no one would connect me with him. I didn't want anyone to know he was my father because I was so ashamed." One day, the girl she happened to sit next to saw the tussle her father was causing at the back of the bus and said, "Who is that man?" Karen responded, "I don't know; I've never seen him before."

When Karen shared her painful story with me, my mind went back to my own home. My father, unlike Karen's, was always home predictably and faithfully. Every Saturday during the fall, we would watch college football games on television. Mother would sew and Pop would make chili. While he cooked, he would dance a little shuffle by the kitchen range and make up silly songs to make us laugh.

Danna Kay and I were always assured of our parents' love. Pop would come into the living room, pinch our cheeks and say, "Your daddy loves you." And he showed it in dozens of ways. But try as we all would, our family could not escape the sadness of watching my father's body be visibly affected by a cruel disease known as neurofibromatosis.

My father was in his thirties when a doctor first told him he had been born with this incurable affliction. Then he was the picture of health and snapshots of him show him dark-haired and handsome. But when he died 27 years later of heart disease at 58, his skin was covered from head to toe with thousands of lumps and tumors. Neurofibromatosis is the disease that marred the life of John Merrick whose life was portrayed in the motion picture "The Elephant Man." He was so disfigured that he lived in seclusion and covered his grossly deformed head with a cloth the few times he ventured out in public.

I remember walking in public places with my father who always kept his eyes on the ground, hoping not to see the glances and the fixed gazes of people who had never seen anyone like him before. I would anxiously scan the faces of passersby, wondering if they noticed and hoping they wouldn't. I was afraid my schoolmates would see him and reject him, and one day, like Karen, my worst fear was realized.

Pop had come to pick me up from school to take me somewhere. He was walking a few feet in front of me when one of my high school acquaintances pointed at Pop and said, "Look! That man has leprosy!" I turned on her, shocked and angry, and said, "That's my father!" and she hurried away. And to this day whenever I see someone handicapped or afflicted, I pay them the highest compliment I can: I never look twice.

We talked about it so seldom that as I am writing this I have to look up the word in the dictionary to check the spelling. I don't know when Pop realized how devastating the disease would be. But the lumps that covered his body also scarred our feelings. We had our church friends, but I can count on one hand the times other families outside of ours came for dinner. My parents were never invited to parties, and Mother's social life was confined to friendships with other teachers at school. Pop had friends at work who enjoyed his company because, as is the case with other afflicted and handicapped people, those who grow accustomed to seeing them go beyond externals and don't think twice about it. But no one but Mother, Danna Kay and I ever saw enough of Pop to know how beautiful he was, to know that tears would fill his eyes when he heard that tragedies had befallen others and how he would weep at the pictures of Vietnam on the evening news. No one saw him study the Bible every night or gave him the chance to teach a Sunday school class, even though he was well-prepared. Few people want to be around those who make them feel uncomfortable, who remind them that life is fragile, sometimes hopelessly painful, and that healthy people can become victims.

Our family was constantly reminded with sadness that we were different, even though we didn't want to be. No medicine, no stay in a treatment center, no attendance at a support group could counteract the cruel fact that Pop would only become more disfigured and never be healed—not this side of heaven.

And I was ashamed and afraid of what might happen to Pop or to us. I felt an impulse to defend him and protect his feelings from insensitive people. And because of my Christian upbringing, I was ashamed of feeling ashamed. In my mind I knew that the source of shame was nothing any of us could control, but the reproach remained deeply embedded. I used to wonder why I do the things I do. I laugh and joke to ease emotionally tense situations. I play the hero and work to prove our family is worth something—that we're just as good as everybody else.

I am an adult child, too, and have suffered through every issue in this book: childishness because I had to face a painful reality too young; shame because I felt my family was different; the fear of abandonment and rejection because I wondered if anyone outside my family would really love me; isolation because of my father's affliction; role-playing, mask-wearing, trying to control because during my childhood I was a victim of what we couldn't change; low self-esteem and perfectionism that make me want to prove my worth. Nothing eased my pain until five years ago when God began to lift my head and show me how to get rid of the awful residue that clung to me. I will share with you how my healing is progressing, but first, let's take a look at shame.

When we sin, we ought to feel shame. It is a warning that we have overstepped the boundaries and have violated our consciences. Shame is the central emotion that helps develop a conscience; and guilt is unresolved, leftover shame that afflicts our consciences until we say we are sorry and determine not to repeat the sin.

Shame is not only an emotion but also the spiritual state of being for those who do not have God's covering for their sins—the blood of Jesus Christ. This sense of shame is a manifestation of the mercy of God because it opens up the person to receiving God's cover for his sin. This is all healthy shame.

The shame that afflicts adult children does not usually have to do with sins committed, although none would deny that adult children are sinners like everyone else. Rather, it is what counselor John Bradshaw calls toxic shame. And it afflicts Christians who are already covered with the blood of Jesus Christ and should not feel the torment of shame. "Shame as a healthy human emotion can be transformed into shame as a state of being. As a state of being, shame takes over one's whole identity. To have shame as an identity is to believe that one's being is flawed, that one is defective as a human being. Once shame is transformed into an identity, it becomes toxic and dehumanizing" (*Healing the Shame that Binds You*). It is toxic shame that has the capacity to destroy by motivating the adult child continually to find ways to cover the "nakedness" that comes from feeling flawed and defective.

At the heart of every issue we have mentioned is the sense of unhealthy shame that nags at the emotions, ever whispering the devil's accusation: "Shame on you. You are different, less, defective, inferior." This voice plays over and over in the subconscious mind when we feel the emotion of shame, even over things beyond our control.

We can hear this only so long before we must initiate some act to remove this notion. It is then that the adult child—like Adam and Eve—strips his own fig leaves off the branches and effects a cover-up, a substitute for glory, something to hide the shame of nakedness and vulnerability.

All human effort outside of joyful obedience to Jesus Christ is the pursuit of cover-ups for the sense of shame we feel. These cover-ups are not the shame itself, but the substitutes for shame's antithesis, honor. What Adam lost at the Fall was the sense of honor and dignity that came from the accurate perception of himself as the prize of God's creation. Before the Fall, man was not proud in thinking he was perfect; it was true. But when sin entered him, he became imperfect and fell under the reproach of his own conscience. We still struggle to see ourselves the way God does, to rid ourselves of the idea that God doesn't love us or to escape the unmerciful scrutiny of others who we feel will remind us of our shame by refusing to validate us.

In order to escape their gaze, ashamed people isolate, act, pretend and deny. Pride itself is the result of these inventions. The desire to be restored to honor becomes a lust to be honored, which stops at nothing to obtain the position that we think will erase the sense of shame. Let's look at the following issues that afflict adult children and isolate their roots of shame.

1) Roles

All the roles assumed by members of the dysfunctional home are coping strategies to deal with shame. The hero works hard to restore his sense of self-worth, which was removed when he became aware of the shame-producing dysfunction in his home. The caretaker covers his sense of shame by deeds of rescue and kindness. The lost child copes with shame by fantasizing a new world in which happiness, friendship and peace affirm him. The mascot covers his and the family's sense of shame by laughter and minimization, trying to take the sting out by using other more positive emotions. The scapegoat takes upon himself the focused shame of the family.

2) Masks

Masks are the false faces that people wear to hide the naked-ness they feel. The preoccupation with clothing to change one's appearance is directly related to the need to feel as good as others appear. The preoccupation with wealth, position, accomplish-ment and external beauty is a cover for shame, but so is the untidy appearance of the person whose shame has caused him to give up.

Emotions or the denial of them is another mask. Effecting joy and happiness when you are sad and depressed, disguising anger so that others won't see the childish you, and crying tears to cover for the feeling of unconcern are all false faces assumed to keep from feeling the shame that you cannot rise to the occasion.

3) Positions

In order to appear honorable, human beings lust for positions as James and John lusted for the right- and left-hand seats near Jesus' heavenly throne (Mark 10:37). Somehow we feel that if we can clothe ourselves with a title, we will be validated as persons, that our sense of inadequacy will disappear. In the church, people aspire to ministries that distinguish them from others.

People who seem to have an exalted view of themselves or view themselves as the center of attention are actually ashamed people overcompensating. The ultimate of this is narcissistic personality disorder—the preoccupation with self, which mani-fests itself in grandiosity, control of others and a distorted view of reality. A counselor once told me that should a narcissist come to church, within a matter of days he would move from visitor status to front pew insider, attempting to effect changes to suit his desires. Before Jim Bakker was sent to prison, the court-appointed psychiatrist diagnosed him as having narcissistic personality disorder.

4) Acting

In addition to the roles typical in the dysfunctional home, ashamed people act out false identities, effect mannerisms and speech, and play out roles of persons they admire in order to escape the shame of being themselves. Nowhere is this more evident than in the church where certain postures are considered "holy" or "anointed." Inside the powerful pulpiteer grandstanding to the congregation is usually a frightened child projecting an image he thinks will make others accept him. Sometimes people act out roles they know others will love because they "know" they are unlovable, uninteresting and, therefore, flawed.

5) Envy

Envious people wish they or their circumstances were different so that they could have better advantages than they presently possess. A sense of shame causes them to believe that changes like better jobs or different peer groups would make them more like those they admire and they would no longer feel inferior. A person who is ashamed does not possess the sense of contentment that comes from satisfaction.

Breaking Shame's Secret Strength

Shame remains long after the original source is removed. I haven't seen my father since November 24, 1972, the night before he died, but the sense of false shame, of feeling flawed as a family, remains in my emotions. I can still feel the emotion even though my father is gone.

If the source is removed, why doesn't the pain subside? The answer is that unresolved grief associated with shame remains deeply embedded in the subconscious mind as if locked in a dark closet. Shame gathers its strength and power to destroy the present through silence and secrecy. The fear of disclosure magnifies the emotional pain so that all care is given to ensure that the source of shame remains a secret. This is especially true if a person is ashamed of feeling ashamed. The fear of disclosing his feelings, he thinks, would shame him further.

But the truth is that disclosure to God and other individuals who will sympathize with and validate the feelings of shame is the exact thing that brings release and healing. Maybe you have heard the folk proverb "Tell the truth and shame the devil." One friend said this frequently in high school and I have often marveled at its truth. Breaking the traditions of silence and isolation that surround shame exposes this fraudulent creature for what it is, a counterfeit. Here are some steps that will help.

1) Opening Up

Toxic shame falls away from the Christian as he is transformed by renewing his mind. The Holy Spirit bubbles up like a fountain inside and waters the surrounding desert with the truth about his spiritual condition. The Holy Spirit gradually restores the soul, prompting the believer to take certain steps that will enhance the Spirit's working. The first step in taking the sting out of shame is talking about its source.

Before Adam and Eve could be clothed with the skins God provided, they had to give up their fig leaf substitutes. Opening the source of shame to the light, admitting to God, to yourself and other human beings that you feel ashamed about certain facts, events or perceptions, opens the wound to light and air. Before, it was festering in the closet, sore and painful, but now it is exposed and healing can begin.

My sorrow over my father's affliction lasted for thirteen years after his death. I lived with a strange fear that my Christian friends would find out—as though they would think I were an awful person. I ventured out a little, finally, and told a close girlfriend. I was amazed to see her sympathy and understanding rather than the frozen faces I had seen on the people who saw my father for the first time. I felt relieved. My worst secret was out of the darkness and I did not have to work to keep it in hiding.

Then I told another person and another and another. Then I mentioned it in a sermon I preached and during a testimony at a service. Each time I told how I felt. An important part of releasing the burden is describing your feelings and allowing your emotions to be expressed. Adult children can relate some of the most shameful and frightening events with stoic expressions because their emotions have been shut down. When sharing your sources of shame, let your emotions go. The tears—and even laughter over less serious shameful events like having your fly unzipped or your slip hanging down before an audience—will bring healing. Each time I shared my pain with others, I found acceptance and validation from those outside my family, the very things I was deprived of as a child growing up.

2) Using It as a Building Block

As I shared openly, I found the second step in recovering from shame: using the source of shame as a building block for the rest of your life, turning it into a source of blessing rather than the curse it has always been. Joseph of the Old Testament saw that the tragedies of his life had all worked together to bring to pass his highest good. To his repentant brothers who had sold him into slavery as a youth, he said, "As for you, you meant evil against me, but God meant it for good . . . to preserve many people alive" (Genesis 50:20). Which is another way of saying, "God causes all things to work together for good to those who love God, to those who are called according to His purpose" (Romans 8:28).

This is the beauty of the redeemed life—that God can make beauty out of ugliness, triumph out of tragedy and life out of death. Now, rather than looming like a giant of my past, shame over my father's uncontrollable disease is a foe that God has subdued and put under my feet.

3) Helping Others

There is one more step to taking the sting out of shame. As with every other principle in the Bible, there exists the divine paradox that in order to receive, you need to give. I discovered through my pain that I could become a vessel for bestowing honor on others. We live in a world of hurting people who, in order to compensate for their own sense of shame, steal the glory from others. We belittle and criticize. Often in the church we disrobe the brethren in the name of discernment—knowing good and evil—by stealing the honor that comes from having a good name or the privilege of having their own shameful feelings validated.

Whereas the devil wants to bring reproach, children of the Almighty follow in the image of their heavenly Father whose impulse is to clothe and restore. I am not advocating here be-coming a part of someone's denial system by reinforcing decep-tion in his life.

What I am advocating is bestowing honor, lifting up the heads of the brethren, surrounding them with an atmosphere of unconditional love and acceptance. "With humility of mind let each of you regard one another as more important than himself" (Philippians 2:3). Not only does this encourage the brethren, but it does wonders for our humility. Rather than destroying our self-esteem and multiplying our shame, learning to bless rather than curse, to support rather than abandon, to cover rather than strip, to compliment rather than condemn, raises the position of our brother in our eyes and in his. Surrounding the once shame-based brethren with constant reminders of who they really are in Christ provides an atmosphere in which healing can take place. Praise the honest brother for opening his painful past to the light. Validate his pain by saying, "I understand. I've been there, too."

Another way of bestowing the blessing of honor is through touching. Gary Smalley and John Trent in their bestselling Christian book *The Blessing* wrote: "Touch from both a mother and father is important . . . meaningful touching can protect a child from looking to meet his need in all the wrong places. If we ignore the physical and emotional needs our children, spouse, or close friends have for meaningful touch, we deny them an important part of the blessing." So many adult children have been touched in the wrong way—slapped, beaten, molested sexually. One way God reaches out His hand to touch others is through you. I have often worried about the single adults and widow(er)s in our congregation who have no one to touch and hug them.

When touch is employed in a godly way, it can do wonders for affirming and strengthening the brethren. It is no wonder that the Bible speaks often of the laying on of hands. The patriarchs laid hands on their children and pronounced blessings. Jesus laid His hands on the children who gathered around Him and blessed them, and the early Church employed the laying on of hands for healing and ordination for ministry. The blessings of God—spiritual and emotional—are transferred through the hands. Adult children need to be touched in an affirming way—a kind hand on the shoulder, a pat on the back and a "holy hug." When it is coupled with edifying words of praise and encouragement, touching soothes the anxious soul, which fears loneliness more than anything else.

Years ago as Bill and I began to read about the plight of adult children, we wondered naïvely if anyone in our congregation might be affected. The Scripture kept coming to our minds: "They have healed the wound of My people slightly, saying, 'Peace, peace,' But there is no peace" (Jeremiah 6:14). As we prayed for guidance, we began a series of teachings on Sunday nights about adult children of alcoholics. Attendance was record-breaking and we wondered why until we discovered—as I have relayed elsewhere—that ninety percent of the adults in our church were children of alcoholics and many of those remaining were victims of other forms of direct abuse. We began learning to drop our religious masks and share our pain openly and honestly in the light of God's mercy. And today the subjects that once struck fear in their hearts no longer carry for them the sting of shame. Before, their wounds held them as adult children of alcoholics; now they are children of the Almighty and are beginning to *feel* like it.

Are you starting to feel a sense of hope? As you begin to implement the solutions suggested in this book, you will slowly move toward health. But let's not stop here. Let's move on to the next all-important step in recovering from the wounds of a dysfunctional home.

10
Lord, Help Me to Trust

One of the central issues of adult children is their inability to trust God or anyone easily. Before we look at the issue of trust, take a pencil and answer *yes* or *no*, true or false to the following questions:

_____ 1. Do you find it difficult to let others lead without trying to control, advise or manage?

_____ 2. Do you anticipate that negative events will follow blessings in your life?

_____ 3. Do you usually follow the motto "Don't count your chickens before they are hatched"?

_____ 4. Do you believe that truly capable leaders with integrity are difficult to find today?

_____ 5. Do you maintain contact with several close friends whom you have known for many years?

_____ 6. Do you seek the counsel of other mature persons and try to follow their advice when it's time to make important decisions in your life?

_____ 7. Are you unusually watchful, looking out for signs of trouble before they happen?

_____ 8. True or false: If someone really gets to know you, he or she won't like you.

_____ 9. Answer _committed_ or _change_: Have you been committed actively to the same local church for many years or do you change churches often?

_____ 10. Are you (were you) afraid you might marry the wrong person and wind up unhappy?

_____ 11. True or false: You can't afford to get too close to people.

_____ 12. Answer optimistic or pessimistic: Are you optimistic or pessimistic about the outcome of your life?

_____ 13. Are you often suspicious of the motives of others?

_____ 14. Do you have a generally negative opinion of the opposite sex?

_____ 15. Do you sometimes believe your salvation is in jeopardy?

_____ 16. Do you possess any unfounded fears, such as fear of tragedies befalling you or your loved ones, fear of sickness or death, fear of the dark, fear of heights, claustrophobia, etc.?

_____ 17. Answer afraid or enjoy: Are you generally afraid of people or do you enjoy being around people and developing new friendships?

_____ 18. Is it easy for you to give money to help others, to buy things you need or to tithe to your church?

Score: People who have problems trusting others generally answer this way: _yes_ to questions 1–4, 7, 8, 10 and 13–16; _no_ to questions 5, 6 and 18; _true_ to questions 8 and 11; _pessimistic_ to 12; _afraid_ to 17; and _change_ to number 9. If you answered this way to six or fewer you are doing well at learning to trust; from six to nine you could benefit by some work; more than nine and it would appear you need to concentrate on this area with prayer, counseling and a support group because you are a person who doesn't trust easily.

The Power of Fear to Control

Learning to trust is one of the most basic issues an adult child will face. His past is usually littered with experiences of betrayal, abuse, rejection and lack of approval and affirmation. These experiences produced several dark fears that unless recognized and handled properly can determine the parameters for his life. The following story illustrates the power of these fears to paralyze an adult child's ability to trust.

At the turn of the century Sean O'Reilly's grandparents immigrated to Pittsburgh from Ireland. His grandfather labored at a hazardous job in a steel mill near the open hearth, which sometimes claimed the lives of workers when the furnace's flames would break out. Sean's grandmother worked as a maid, determining never to have to search through garbage cans for food again as they had when they first immigrated to America.

Sean's grandpa was a hard worker and always busy, but always chiding and warning his children that money was valuable, that they should save every penny. Sean's father grew up in this tradition, and it became a part of him. He rarely ventured out of the Irish ghetto except to cross the river and do business in downtown Pittsburgh.

By the '50s, the Great Depression was in the past and Sean's father was now working in the mill making a good salary. But the O'Reilly tradition of frugality lingered, even though the barren days that prompted it were long since gone.

Sean's parents saved every penny and there was never anything for fun or amusements—except at the local Irish pub packed with fathers worn out from a hard day at the mill. Their lives centered around home, church and the mill. Their friends were others who existed in the same way. Sean, his brothers and sisters and their playmates grew up hearing the most frightening tales of deprivation and feared the collapse of the economy.

In the late '70s, Sean broke the family church tradition. The charismatic renewal was sweeping through Pittsburgh and Sean became born again and began attending a nondenominational congregation. He was elated at his newfound faith and witnessed to everyone he met. His wife and family followed him in his spiritual search and were overjoyed to see the changes he was experiencing. But one area of Sean's life was difficult to give over to the Lord—the area of giving.

Although he now made a good salary at the steel mill and was probably one of the more well-fixed members of his church, Sean found it hard, if not impossible, to give. For him, taking out his wallet felt the same as going into surgery.

Whenever the offering plate was passed, he put in a couple of dollars, but guilt was beginning to weigh heavy on his mind. His paralysis in the area of giving was beginning to creep out into other areas of his life, advancing a root of bitterness. It was more difficult for him to sense God's presence, and he found himself reading the Bible less and less. He even sought the counsel of the pastor who encouraged him to try tithing to see God's hand in his life, but Sean couldn't.

The Tradition of Survival

What was bothering Sean bothers successive generations of Americans whose ancestors have "made it" by surviving. Likewise, adult children of dysfunctional homes are survivors, having endured emotional, spiritual or physical deprivation or combinations of all three. Here are characteristics that the survivor mentality produces:

1) One of its manifestations is a rigid *independence*. In order to survive in an atmosphere of deprivation, a person becomes hardened and sometimes dehumanized, as was the case with Ann Feldman's father, the Holocaust survivor. Asking others for help when he can barely survive himself is out of the question. Since others cannot help, he must somehow adjust and make it on his own, taking what he can from a world that has almost nothing to offer. To hesitate is to lose a chance that may never come again. Even though Sean's family clung together in a ghetto, the atmosphere of the neighborhood, because it was closed, bred prejudices against the outside world and isolated itself from society. The ghetto prided itself on unity, closeness and camaraderie, but when the chips were down, it was more often than not every man for himself.

The independence created in Sean by the survival tradition hurt his ability to fellowship with others and to make real friends. He was always afraid that he would get so close to people that he would be relieved of some of his money. He set a boundary around himself that ensured this would never happen.

2) Into this atmosphere was introduced the next element of the survivor mentality, *pessimism*. By eternally poking through garbage cans, standing in line all day and finding no bread left, and wearing old hand-me-downs, the survivor begins to believe in his soul that things will always be this way. They will never get better, and he must not trust circumstances or people. Instead, he should anticipate and brace himself for disappointment. Sean was told frequently in anger by his grandparents and parents, "Don't expect help from anyone. No one helped us, and we don't help anyone!" This pessimism created a "faith" that

God and others would not provide or be there when he needed it most, a fear Sean later was forced to confront.

3) Riding on the trail of pessimism is a tendency toward *criticism* whose root is *jealousy*. If I can't have an advantage, why should others have it? Like crabs trying to crawl out of a bucket, each pulls the others down so that no one escapes. Sean's grandparents, although friendly with many, criticized other families mercilessly and envied those who found better trash with which to furnish their homes. Sean found it difficult to rejoice with others who gave testimonies of God's provision at church because he secretly resented their advantages. And because the minister did not sweat at the mill, Sean believed he did not deserve to make a salary comparable to his own and criticized him for it behind his back.

4) This criticism of the pastor was a symptom of another problem that proceeds from lack of trust and the fear of being taken advantage of: the *mistrust of authority*. When others cannot be trusted and God cannot be trusted, then God working through others certainly cannot be trusted.

When a person has been victimized by authority figures—whether parents, bosses, law enforcement officials or ministers—he transfers the feelings about abuses of the past onto those who have any measure of authority over him in the present. Any imposition of authority is resented and stirs up his rebellious nature. He fights against anything he cannot control because he is afraid of losing control and being victimized once again.

In *Grown-Up Abused Children* authors James Leehan and Laura P. Wilson write:

> Grown-up abused children . . . must learn to differentiate people who have authority over them in the present from abusive persons in their past. They must begin to recognize and control the transferences they may be making. . . .

5) Ironically, when advantages are obtained and the need for struggle passes, the *fear of poverty* still lives in a survivor like a cancer in the human soul, cutting off the joy and satisfaction of reward. The fear of poverty causes its victims to save everything —old clothes, utensils, broken appliances—anything that might be of some use if the economy failed or if good fortune once again evaporated. These people become ruled by the fear that poverty will return and shatter the happy dream. In order to cushion the blow, they must be prepared for such eventualities. Hoarding is one way of preparation, but so is the mental game of bracing yourself for dry times.

In spite of his affluence, Sean collected things, too. His basement was loaded with junk that could be "turned into something nice." His wife hoarded food for which they purchased two freezers. Their pantry was maintained with ten cans of each item.

6) In order to brace himself for the wind that might blow it all away, *self-deprivation* must become the underlying philosophy of the survivor's life. Just as the anorexic always sees herself as fat when she is extremely thin, the survivor sees himself as poor when he is usually well-fixed—with insurance policies, savings and investments. Depriving himself of all but the bare necessities is the hallmark of his life. He justifies his stinginess with himself and others as wisdom when it is really the fear of poverty that motivates him.

Even when Sean's father became employed at the mill and the union won them working conditions, salaries and benefits beyond his wildest dreams, he continued to deprive his family. They used the furniture they had pulled from the garbage, always shopped at the cheapest places and rarely indulged in pleasure.

One time, when he was in elementary school, Sean was taken to the local amusement park, but his father griped so much about the expense of the outing that Sean felt guilty at having wanted to go. All forms of amusement were considered frivolous and every expenditure was accompanied by this line: "Do you know how many hours of slavery it took to buy this for you?"

The survivor mentality has created a backlash in modern America. The baby boomer "me" generation has won the tug-of-war with its financially deprived parents and fallen into a muck of materialism. Bucking the idea of self-deprivation, this generation is spending to billion dollar proportions. And it is rearing a new generation equally out of balance in which every whim must be satisfied instantly. And yet the same spiritual emptiness that affected its survivor parents affects the me generation—an emptiness that cannot be filled with comforts, pleasures and possessions.

The survivor mentality also affects the Church. Doctrines of self-abasement and asceticism have always mushroomed during times of persecution and struggle. The belief that it is "holy" to suffer and that deprivation brings a spiritual state in which we are more pleasing to Christ weaves like a thread through many sermons of history's greatest preachers. The one who suffers, however, is more often than not afraid, bitter, resentful and unable to trust God or anyone else. God has left me in the pit, he thinks, and it will be years before He brings me out again, if He ever does. The fear of abandonment underlies the fear of poverty, as it does every other fear.

Sean was spiritually deprived as a result of the economic deprivation that he had learned as a tradition. He never saw God as his source of provision because his own father had provided so stingily. He believed his job was his provider, and he worked hard at it. But one day his worst fear came to pass.

In 1982 the union called a meeting. The Homestead works of U.S. Steel, the main plant whose historic riots more than one hundred years before had led to the development of labor unions, was scheduled for closing. In one moment, Sean was devastated.

Suddenly all the fears created by his childhood crashed in on him.

Surviving Survival

But in the middle of his now-real struggle to survive, Sean finally found the victory many adult children need to learn—that God is their only provider. The Lord took Sean on a pathway that healed him of the survivor mentality and taught him to trust. Here is how He did it.

Learning to Receive

This was Sean's first lesson. The church people who had known little or nothing of Sean's inner struggles about giving rose to his need and began to pour out financial blessings on the O'Reillys. The women organized a food pantry and brought over covered dishes. Sean was humbled that people poorer than himself stopped by his home to console him and press bills into his hand. Little by little his independence was being worn down, although it was very hard for him to take "charity" from anyone. This was mainly because he didn't want to be obliged to give it. In order to change, he had to learn to receive.

We all would like to receive from impersonal sources because it doesn't embarrass or hurt us. The perfectionistic tendency adult children have, which sees life operating by law rather than grace, usually surrounds the one infected with a survivor mentality. His concept of financial blessing is usually punitive: "If God approves of me, He will bless me; but if hard times ensue, it is the punishment of God." Sean had heard this thought creep in several times when he witnessed the misfortunes of others. He surmised only that they had done something wrong to warrant the Lord's frown. When he lost his job, his own words heaped judgment on himself. He wondered why God had allowed this to happen rather than seeing it as a common vicissitude of life. He was thrown into a depression set up by his own pride.

But as the Lord's grace flowed through the members of Sean's church when he deserved, as he thought, a slap on the hand or a deaf ear, Sean was humbled. He became ashamed of having been so hardened and calloused toward others who suffered. Saying "thank you" had never come easy for him, but it began to teach him that blessing was on the basis of grace, not works.

Jesus said, "Freely you have received; freely give." Now that Sean learned how to receive, he was ready for the next step in learning to trust and breaking the stranglehold of the survival mentality.

Learning to Give

This was one lesson he had never learned. Sermons about giving always angered him and he complained that those who taught them were "only out for your money." Being in a position where he either had to receive or not make it showed Sean the joy of being blessed. When he began to open his eyes to the feelings and frustrations of those in need, he found himself wanting to help others escape from the trial he was facing. His compassion got a vitamin shot in the arm, and he began to give out of his lack.

When others shared their griefs at church, he found himself sympathetic and overwhelmed with the desire to help as he had been helped. "When you've got nothin', you've got nothin' to lose!" he found himself joking one day as he wrote out a check to help a brother in need.

Learning to Trust

In the middle of receiving and then giving, something wonderful happened to Sean. He automatically found himself trusting God to meet his needs and the needs of his family. Sometimes there were days of doubt and fear when he wondered if God had seen his plight, but underneath his doubts lay an unshakable confidence that he had done all he could do and now he could trust God. And Sean's new trust did not go unrewarded. During the four years it took to recover from the loss of his job, Sean saw so many miracles of divine provision that he said, "I could write a book!"

Sometimes now when faced with new problems, Sean and his family look back to the way God brought them through that wilderness. Through those memories Sean usually winds up encouraging others going through hard times that God is right there with them and that the provision is just around the corner.

Learning to Bless

Because God is using him to help others in the same difficulty, Sean is learning the final lesson of trust. Learning to bless is becoming his priority. Before he lost his job, he resented the benefits others received, but now he prays that others will receive blessings and advantages! Without realizing it, Sean is breaking a century-old curse on himself and his family by not continuing in the sins that caused it.

Have the windows of heaven opened for Sean? He thinks so. Not only has this seeming horror of losing his job turned into one of his greatest triumphs spiritually, but God has begun to restore Sean's finances. While Sean was still in depression after having lost his job at the mill, he sheepishly sought the pastor for counseling. The pastor suggested he take his unemployment compensation and go back to school. Sean enrolled in college to earn his degree, something no one else in his family had ever done. Four years later he was graduated and now has an entirely new career in the computer field. Instead of sweating on the open hearth in a fireproof suit, he sits at a desk in an air-conditioned office.

"Losing my job at the mill was the best thing that ever happened to me—a real blessing in disguise!" Sean says. "It was God's way of showing me I didn't have to be afraid because He could be trusted to provide better than my earthly father was able to do." Through this experience the survivor mentality has been eradicated from Sean's soul. "Now my favorite part of the service is when the offering plate is passed!" Sean jokes—but maybe he isn't joking after all.

Sean is no longer surviving, he is living. Gone is the fear of poverty. Gone is his pessimistic outlook on life. Sean is moving on to other areas of spiritual development confident that God will help him because His character—not just His power—can be trusted.

In the next chapter, we will look at overcoming the hindrances that keep the adult child from being able to make decisions. Let's read on in our pursuit of the Good Shepherd's healing power.

11

Overcoming a Timid Spirit

Do you do any of the following:

_____ 1. Believe you are not all right?

_____ 2. Feel unlovable, ugly or stupid?

_____ 3. Feel unworthy of friends or of caring from others?

_____ 4. Have difficulty receiving praise or compliments?

_____ 5. Feel incapable of making decisions that govern your life?

_____ 6. Feel out of control of your life?

_____ 7. Seem unable to ask for anything for yourself?

_____ 8. Feel awkward or clumsy?

_____ 9. Gravitate toward other needy people for friendship?

_____ 10. Have difficulty acknowledging and making your feelings known?

_____ 11. Often feel that no one pays attention to you?

_____ 12. Change jobs frequently or have difficulty holding down a job?

_____ 13. Fear failure even though you have been successful in the past?

_____ 14. Believe you can't really have an effect in the world?

_____ 15. Engage in self-sabotage by helping your own plans fall through—quit school or not show up for appointments, for example—in order to confirm your worst fears about yourself?

_____ 16. Believe that good relationships are bound to fail later on?

_____ 17. Brag about your accomplishments or qualities to cover for your insecurities?

_____ 18. Take on responsibilities and then shift them later on when something else comes up?

_____ 19. Feel guilty asserting yourself?

_____ 20. Change your beliefs and opinions quickly when others object, even when you know you are right?

_____ 21. Feel intimidated by assertive people?

_____ 22. Feel at a loss for words when someone asks you what you prefer?

Score: The more answers you checked the more likely you are to have a timid spirit. Let's see what can be done about it.

How It Happens

Perhaps no other attribute paralyzes the adult child more than a timid spirit. The timid spirit is not a spirit of meekness, the gentle characteristic of those led by the Holy Spirit quietly but firmly to do the will of God. The timid spirit is a conquered spirit. It is the emotional state of the soul that has been punished repeatedly for living, breathing and asserting its rightful place in the world.

God has given every person a place, but someone with a timid spirit is constantly taken over by aggressive persons who know how to strike him at his weakest points, fear and passivity. Over and over again, his soul has been invaded by persons and forces outside of itself until he has been left wounded and trampled in the dust. When a country is repeatedly overrun, it loses its identity as a nation, and so does the human soul that has no established fortress to guard it. Anyone with a stronger will and the desire to exert it can overrun a person with a timid spirit and prevent him from doing or thinking what he desires, including pushing him out of the will of God.

What creates a timid spirit? Are people born that way or do events mold this aspect of character? Not to be confused with a naturally quiet temperament, the timid spirit grows from fear and can invade any temperament and influence personality and character. People are not born with timid spirits but are shaped and molded by the environments in which they grew to adulthood.

The dysfunctional home is the perfect breeding ground for the timid spirit because its traditions force the developing child to submit to its aberrant ways. Rigidity and perfectionism in the problem person and his/her spouse cause developing children to be less and less able to assert their own identities and to be less appreciated for the distinct creations they are. They are conformed to a standard created by the unrenewed minds of the controlling individuals in the home and in order to survive must cease to exist emotionally. Vince is a case in point.

Vince grew up the eldest son in an Italian family of three children, one of whom, his sister, died when she was twelve years old. His father followed in the traditions well established by his grandfather and great-grandfather who prided themselves on macho images and the ability to rule their homes with force and domination. Vince's mother was unsure of herself and unable to assert her will against her overbearing husband.

In order to keep his children in line, Vince's father believed that frequent beatings were in order. "I was beaten regularly, several times a week, sometimes hit across the face with my father's leather belt." Rigid rules sometimes differed from day to day, depending on the moods of the parents, so that Vince grew up afraid to step very far in any direction.

Homework was always supervised by their ill-tempered father. He would sit at the table with them making sure every assignment was completed to perfection. He would ask them questions, and if they gave an incorrect or incomplete answer, he would hit them and call them names.

Vince and his brother, Danny, were not rebellious sons. Instead, they were compliant and almost fearful, never venturing their opinions for fear of stirring their father's temper. Their mother never took their side, but would actually encourage their father to beat them harder and more severely.

Negatively conditioned by verbal and physical abuse, Vince and Danny grew up afraid to think or assert their individuality in any way. Vince was in his thirties when he found the girl of his dreams, whose personality happened to be the opposite of his own. Vince was shy, softspoken and unsure of himself. Betsy was aggressive, talkative, fun to be around. They entered married life expecting everything to be fine. And it was—until communication became a problem.

"I didn't know how to treat Betsy," says Vince. "I had never learned how to think for myself and usually mirrored the opinions of others. When Betsy asked me to give my opinion about something first, I was paralyzed, fumbling for words." It was then that Vince realized he didn't know what he liked, disliked or thought about anything. He was not used to forming opinions and often swayed with the direction the wind seemed to be blowing those around him. He felt as though there was little definition to his personality. He feared making decisions because he had never learned the art; and now, forced into the role as head of his household, Vince was afraid he couldn't please Betsy—that he would bore her.

Vince's timidity was the direct result of the negative conditioning he received as a child. When a person is punished or chided for being himself, he develops a sense of shame about the way God made him. Conditioned to believe that he is flawed, the abused person becomes afraid to form opinions and assert his preferences. If he is flawed, then his ideas must also be flawed. This belief usually further perverts itself until the victim believes he is bad and carries on his shoulders a load of projected false guilt for taking up air and standing room from those who are more worthy to be alive. Here are expressions of behavior in an adult child with a timid spirit.

Fear of Others

This expression is one I mentioned earlier. The timid person fears others. And the "fear of man," according to Proverbs 29:25, brings a snare. It leads to sin because it displaces God's will as top priority with subservience to controlling individuals.

The apostle Paul wrote: "If I were still trying to please men, I would not be a bond-servant of Christ" (Galatians 1:10). Although Paul maintained a submissive spirit, he was often required to stand for truth against an overwhelming tide of public opinion. We have Paul to thank that the heresy of the Judaizers did not permeate the Church. He even had to stand his ground against Peter. If Paul had been a man-pleaser instead of a God-pleaser, we would still be in bondage to the Law of Moses. Sometimes we, too, must stand against temptation and public opinion. Anyone with a timid spirit has difficulty with this.

Fear of Failure

Another expression of the timid spirit is a fear of failure. The one who is unsure of himself and disparages his own ideas and opinions will never attempt to launch out and try anything new. The possibility of not succeeding will keep him bound. He may fear what people will think of him if he fails. He may also fear that he will not please God. The bottom line is that he is really afraid of disappointing himself.

Inability to Make Decisions

Like Vince, adult children often have to make decisions without knowing the proper guidelines for observing and calculating different solutions. They have not learned the effective process for making decisions, so that much of what they wind up deciding is poorly planned and results in their much-feared failure. This leads to further fear and inability to decide.

In abusive homes, the rules and decisions are made by parents whose moods and feelings alter from moment to moment. What was a rigid rule one day becomes unenforced the next, so that the growing child is kept guessing at what appropriate behavior really is. When parents continually change the ground rules, children grow up uneasy and feel as though they are running through a minefield where the ground underneath, which is supposed to sustain them, could explode at any moment.

Gideon was the son of an idolater, a Baal worshiper, and although we don't know about the climate of his home, we do know that he considered himself an unlikely candidate to be the "valiant warrior" the angel of the Lord said he was. When God called Gideon to become a judge of Israel and lead the Israelites into battle against Midian, Gideon's initial reaction was disbelief and anger that God would impose such a task on him. His timid spirit was manifested in the inability to make a clear-cut decision about what God was really asking him to do. Not sure he had seen the "right" vision and heard the "right" words, Gideon placed a fleece before the Lord and on successive nights asked God to show him a sign by making the ground wet and the fleece dry . . . then the fleece wet and the ground dry. The night before battle Gideon was still uncertain of his divine mandate and asked for another sign. Not until he overheard the enemy talking about him in fearful tones did he realize that God was truly calling him to victory over the Midianites. His indecisiveness revealed his timid spirit.

Passivity

When a child grows up believing that he is incapable of making an effective decision, he comes to believe that he cannot change anything or have any positive effect on his environment so he may give up and become passive.

The passive or passive-aggressive person is full of unresolved anger at circumstances beyond his control. He is usually intimidated by stronger, more confident people and finds passive ways to resist them. If he is married to an ebullient mate, the passive-aggressive will clam up rather than talk to get his point across or lie down on the couch and unfold the newspaper until the storm blows over. He feels incapable of holding his own in an argument where quick tongues mean the advantage, so he copes by his silence.

But passivity goes beyond clamming up during an argument. It is possible to adopt an entirely passive approach to life. No goals are set, no circumstances are resisted and anyone who is more aggressive is allowed to overrule his wishes and implement theirs. This causes the timid person to become depressed cyclically because he always comes around to a situation he is afraid to handle. His fears rise up and thwart what few plans he does make, so he turns his anger in on himself and sulks. Afraid of failing, afraid of deciding and afraid he will always stay in this state, the timid person becomes paralyzed with immobility, the ultimate passive state. He sits in front of the T.V. or gives in to other addictive-compulsive behaviors to distract himself from decisions he knows he must make.

Moses was living in a relatively passive state when God reached down and called him out of the desert of Midian to go lead the Israelites out of Egypt. For forty years Moses had been living the quiet life of a shepherd, watching his father-in-law's sheep and enjoying family life. He had completely forgotten about the oppression of the Hebrews by their Egyptian captors and seemed to be relieved that he had escaped the wrath of the Pharaoh. He had no goals for life beyond tending sheep when God appeared to him in the burning bush. In order to get Moses to obey Him, God had to transform his timid spirit with repeated signs and assurances that He would go with Moses to Egypt and give him victory.

Bravado

The timid person sometimes covers his timidity and feelings of inadequacy with bravado. He is the expert, always rising to the crisis, managing others on the scene. This self-assertiveness is a substitute for true spiritual boldness and is a mask for a deep sense of inadequacy, which tells the sufferer that he is really a failure when the chips are down.

Simon Peter's mouth was always open in every place he appears in Scripture. His natural temperament dictated his tendency to talk, but what came out of his mouth were usually confident assertions that amounted to no more than empty boasting. Jesus knew this and warned him the night before His crucifixion that in spite of his promised loyalty, he would deny his Master three times before the night was over. Indeed, this prophecy came to pass within hours, and Simon Peter fled from the scene of Jesus' trial a broken man.

Compromise

Another expression of a timid spirit is the tendency to compromise important beliefs to gain the sympathy and approval of

others. The timid person desperately needs affirmation from others and fears continually what they will do to him if he does not
comply and please.

King Saul was an outstanding example of someone who lost
the anointing of God because his fear of what the people thought
led him to compromise. Rather than wait for the prophet Samuel
to show up at the battle scene for the offering, the fearful King
Saul, afraid that God would not send Samuel in time to keep the
people from turning against him, offered the sacrifice himself.
But attempting to maintain the confidence of the people by
disobeying God caused Saul ultimately to lose his position, his
sanity and his life. In Saul's case, his timid spirit was fatal.

Failure to Stick It Out

The final expression of timidity is this: Adult children are
noted for letting you down at the last minute and, as we have
seen, have trouble seeing projects through from beginning to
end. Possibly because they have been repeatedly disappointed
themselves by authority figures and have been promised things
and never received them, they have learned to cop out in the
home stretch. Another factor in the development of this character flaw is compulsivity, the nature of addicts, which is also
seen in their children. The compulsive person makes promises in
a fit of excitement but runs out of the fuel necessary to carry
them out.

Before Elisha the prophet died, he called King Joash to his side
and instructed him to take a handful of arrows and strike the
ground with them to show how serious he was about defeating
the king of Aram. Joash took the arrows and struck the ground
only three times. Elisha rebuked him for not striking more so
that he might also have struck Aram until he destroyed it.

Joash gave up too soon. Whether he struck compulsively or

struck out of a spirit of timidity and fear, unsure of what he should do, the results were the same. He failed to strike until he conquered.

Likewise, the children of Israel in the Promised Land failed to drive out all the inhabitants of the land, Saul failed to purge the land of the Amalekites, the disciples all fell away from Jesus and other Bible characters "pooped out" before the job was done.

Those who work with adult children can find this one of the most frustrating points about their character. They often promise to take on responsibilities and vow they will complete projects begun, but before long when something else they would rather do comes up, they try to shift the responsibility and leave the more conscientious persons holding the bag.

One of the reasons they fail to see projects through may be rooted in their need to be continually exhorted. When self-esteem is damaged, the soul is wounded and incapable of strengthening itself by recalling what God has said, what the Scriptures teach or the encouragement already received. The feelings of inadequacy tend to dominate rather than the voice of the Holy Spirit within. Those who try to encourage adult children find themselves pouring encouragement into a bag with holes created by past emotional wounds. As a result, the adult child needs continual exhortation and encouragement to complete what he has vowed to start.

These expressions of behavior would, it seems, make the person with a timid spirit less effective as a leader. So isn't it interesting how the Lord chose the timid people mentioned here to be His leaders? God's callings are not based on temperament and fleshly characteristics, but on His divine grace.

What He has done with these leaders provides the secrets adult children need to learn in order to overcome a timid spirit and stretch out of the mold into which their dysfunctional homes have conformed them. When Paul wrote his letters to young Timothy, he exhorted him to be strong in the faith, to stand his ground in his heavenly calling, to stir up the supernatural gifts of God he had received at his ordination to ministry. And then he wrote, "For God has not given us a spirit of timidity, but of power and love and discipline" (2 Timothy 1:7). One of the first things God did for each timid person He used was to give them confidence that He was with them and would not leave them.

Overcoming Fright

The timid person is fearful of being pushed into a situation he cannot handle without the resources to deal with it. As we have seen, several factors contribute to this. The adult child has been repeatedly disappointed and abandoned in situations in which he felt unprotected and vulnerable. Having never been taught the resources to survive, he has taught himself different coping strategies in which he feels little confidence. He simply doesn't know if the way he handles life's situations is acceptable. Things could fall apart and leave him once again vulnerable to those who are wiser or more knowledgeable, more assertive or powerful. His fears are usually not based in fact, but then, what fear is? All people are insecure about certain things and fear is a natural response to strange situations. What the adult child needs if he is to embolden himself and fulfill the will of God for his life is to know that God loves him and will be right here with him holding his hand to ward off those who would prey upon his vulnerability.

Let's look a little more closely at Moses' situation.

When God called Moses to shepherd Israel out of the clutches of Pharaoh, Moses was reluctant, voicing fear after fear to the Almighty. "Who am I that I should go to Pharaoh and deliver the sons of Israel out of Egypt?" was Moses' first question. But God responded as though Moses had really said, "God, I'm scared to go down there all by myself!"

God said, "Certainly I will be with you."

Moses' next protest was in essence, "What if I tell them the God of Abraham, Isaac and Jacob sent me and then they ask me what Your name is? I don't know You very well!" Again God reassured Moses by telling him His name and His reason for wanting to deliver them.

Then Moses voiced another fear common to all timid persons: "What if they won't believe me or listen to what I say?" God responded by giving Moses miraculous signs and powers to demonstrate his calling. Moses raised another objection: "I can't speak well enough."

God reassured Moses again. "Who made mouths, anyway? Wasn't it My idea in the first place? Now go on and I will be with your mouth."

Still Moses could not believe it. He finally raised God's ire by saying, "Pick someone else to speak." God allowed Aaron, Moses' brother, to be the spokesman, but it wasn't His first choice and Aaron made trouble for Moses later on.

God assured Moses repeatedly that He would accompany him, would not leave him, would help him. Almost like a mother urging her timid child onto the playground, God urged Moses out of his secure nest and into the arena of life in His will. This is true of every instance in the Bible in which God called a timid person. He gave repeated assurances of His love, His presence and His power. The timid individual cannot let go without God's dealing a fatal blow to his fear of abandonment.

Moses finally learned to let go of his timid spirit. Later on in the book of Exodus, it is astounding to see Moses go nose to nose with Pharaoh, the most powerful ruler on earth at the time, and not back down. His understanding of the continual presence of God and confidence in His supernatural power turned Moses into a warrior.

Whenever God calls adult children into ministry, He spends a lot of time comforting and reassuring them of His continual presence. Their worst fear is that God will abandon them in the clinch, but this is not the God we serve.

If you as an adult child allow His comforting words to spring up in your heart and water your thirsty soul with the assurance of His love, His presence and His power, you will lose timidity in the face of confidence. And not only does God promise to be with you, but He will give you sound judgment, the supernatural ability to find out the will of God so that you may carry it out boldly.

After assuring you of His presence and overcoming your fears, the other thing God will do before He sends you into scary places is teach you how to make decisions. Let's examine this principle in Vince's life.

Learning How to Decide

Vince shared with me that the hardest decision he ever had to make was whether or not to remove his father's life support system. Vince's father was made an invalid for twelve years by a stroke, but the last stroke had left him brain-damaged and incapable of surviving without the mechanical life support system.

"I had never made a decision in my life about the smallest detail. But there I was in the emergency room, surrounded by the doctors, nurses, my brother and mother and my other family members who were all looking at me as the elder son to make this crucial decision." Fortunately for Vince, he had become a Christian several years before this fateful day and had spent the last few years talking to his father about Jesus Christ. Not long before his father lapsed into the coma from which he never regained consciousness, Vince was able to lead his father, who had so abused him, to the Lord. He died peacefully as Vince gave his permission to remove the life support system.

Every decision you make has the potential to alter the course of your life. This is an awesome thought, but to the person who is afraid of making a decision, this knowledge is paralyzing.

Vince found at that moment the equipment he needed to make a good decision. Let's look at the factors that undergirded him and see how you might apply them to your life as well.

In order to keep your life under the guidance of the Holy Spirit, it is necessary to obtain wisdom from God in your decision-making. "Many are the plans in a man's heart, but the counsel of the Lord, it will stand" (Proverbs 19:21). The Lord can sort through all your ideas and proposed solutions and begin to lead you in the right direction if you commit the decision to Him. In order to do this, pray for wisdom and guidance from the Lord. As the Good Shepherd, Jesus Christ wants nothing better than to lead you into righteousness. One of His missions as Messiah is to "guide our feet into the way of peace." It is not God's will that you timidly stumble and fumble through life unable to make decisions and carry them out. He wants to lead you on the right path for His reputation's sake. God will take responsibility for the circumstances of your life and the outcome of decisions made in an honest attempt to find out His will. If you have trouble believing that God will show you what to do, you need to study the nature and character of your loving Father.

The next step after praying to know God's will is laying down your own will. This is not always easy, but when you realize that God does not always demand sacrifice and is not interested in punishing you for your wants or desires, it is easier to let go of your own preconceived plans. Letting go of your own will clears the conscience so that when you receive an understanding of God's will, you will not be racked with internal conflict—"Is this God, me or the devil?"

Letting go means submitting your plans and desires to change.

Rigidly established borders must sometimes move two or three inches to accommodate the new situation. The rigid person will always experience difficulty in decision-making and try to pigeonhole every new circumstance into his neatly formed boxes. Many things, however, cannot be plugged in so easily. Be open to being changed, to letting go of fears and saying yes sometimes instead of no all the time. The person who says yes all the time may need to start saying no, and this also means submitting to change. Sometimes letting go of your own will means postponing the fulfillment of your desires temporarily so that the will of God may come first.

When making decisions, it is necessary to determine whether or not you are making an emotional decision or a rational one. We cannot—and should not—shut down our emotions but must all the same take a long, honest look at motive. Sometimes motives are hard to decipher. Perhaps the question is this: Should your emotions be given priority? Does what you want interfere with the well-being of others? Notice I did not say with the *desires* of others. The person who always gives in to the desires of others, when they are selfish, does himself and others great harm. He becomes manipulated and controlled.

Vince's emotions were a swirl of confusion. On the one hand—the deep-seated emotional one—he had suffered years of shattering pain from this man. On the other hand, he had forgiven his father and found great joy in leading him to Christ. He realized he did not want to let his father go—certainly a stunning witness to the depths of Jesus' healing power!—but he had to consider his father's well-being and realize it was time to release him.

It is important to note that laying down your will does not always mean that your desires are outside of God's. I believe that God steers the faithful Christian through—not apart from—his desires. Our desires are affected by many factors including our perception of God and ourselves. The person who thinks God is an abusive Father will be afraid to choose any delightful course of action, assuming that God would not want him to have pleasure or that he himself is so wicked as to always choose what is wrong. If you are afraid God will judge you for your decision, ask yourself whether or not you feel that way because it is against His revealed will in Scripture or because of your veiled perception of His love and grace.

The next step after praying to know God's will and laying down your own will is actually discovering God's will. Many ideas and possible solutions may flood your mind at this time and snatches of all of them may be puzzle pieces to God's panorama for your life. The perfectionist would like a written sheet of instructions to float down from on high, but God has designed the human brain as His message center. How will you know that what you are thinking is God's will? The answer is found in the book of James: "The wisdom from above is first pure, then peaceable, gentle, reasonable, full of mercy and good fruits, unwavering, without hypocrisy" (James 3:17). Will your idea pass through this sieve?

One of the main qualities of God's will, for instance, is that it is reasonable. Sometimes Christians impulsively choose to follow certain courses because of voices they hear or ideas they have compelling them to do strange things. They construe these voices to be God, but is what they suggest reasonable? If not, the author of confusion is speaking, not the God of peace. If you feel guilty, driven and pushed, disturbed within, or if an action would bring forth fruit contrary to what God would desire, set it aside for now and choose the course that most fits the other criteria.

Maybe your idea is not all wrong—only partially cluttered with selfish ambition. The perfectionist will tend to throw out the whole idea if he sees a flaw and become stalled in his attempt to find the will of God. If you discover flaws when you pass your plans through this sieve, ask for God's forgiveness and go on trusting Him to change you as you release it to Him.

When you are deciding on a course of action remember to look for these three things: God's will, God's way and God's time. God's will always withstands the litmus test of the fruit of the Holy Spirit, God's way is always full of integrity and usually requires faith to trust Him to see you through and God's time is rarely ever in a rush. Our Father is on an eternal, timeless clock. He is not rushed and hurried and does not want you to feel pressured into making a decision about which you have no peace.

"Let the peace of Christ rule in your hearts" (Colossians 3:15) means just that. The word *rule* is the word *brabeuo*, which means "to act as umpire." Anyone who has ever watched major league baseball knows that regardless of what we think in the stands, the umpire is boss on the field. What he says is what it is. So it is with the wisdom of God. It should create peace and a clear conscience. If it doesn't, wait. The reason why will be revealed shortly. What if people think you're crazy? Tough. If the peace of God calls "foul" all you have to say is, "I just don't have peace about it." That's one of the fringe benefits of being God's child. You can put a lot of things off on "My daddy won't let me." Sometimes postponing a decision is necessary. The circumstances may adjust themselves, the motives of hearts may be revealed and things that are emergencies today usually work out without a lot of frantic phone-calling and stir. Then when you have peace in your heart, it is easy to choose a course of action within moments. When your plan meets the criteria of God's will, God's way and God's time, you can be reasonably certain that you have seen the markers that point you toward God's plan for your life.

All that is left then is to ask God to steer you as you move. The person trying to steer a car parked in a garage gets nowhere. But once you are moving, the scenery changes and new options present themselves that you never saw until you backed out of the driveway. One benefit of moving is that you can usually turn around and go back to the previous exit if you make a wrong turn or lose your way, but at least you are out of the garage of indecision.

As you start making decisions and forming opinions you will begin to feel more confident by asserting yourself as one who is allowed to influence others around you. Rather than resorting to methods of dysfunctional communication to manipulate or to sit by passively while others live life, you will gain more confidence by making decisions and discovering that you are very often right. But what if you are wrong?

Being wrong is also part of living and deciding. Even in spite of our efforts to determine what God's will is, we may not always know. Sometimes we must decide on the basis of what options are presently open, and we get the impression that God does not have a preference in the matter. In such cases, make a choice based on where you are now. God will take you from where you are into His will should you make a mistake. Very often you will never know if you made a mistake because God will redeem it and weave it into the fabric of your life.

Overcoming a timid spirit with the assurance of God's love, power and the ability to determine the mind of God and possess sound judgment is a major step in healing the wounded soul of the adult child. As in other issues facing the adult child, this healing is likely not to be a one-time event, but a series of events that set up the healing process with opportunities for learning and growing. Several situations in your life may increase your faith and confidence in God and in His ability to work through you so that as you grow old, you will wear a crown of wisdom in place of the spirit of timidity.

Now let's move on to another step in restoring the wounded soul of the adult child.

12
How to Stop Running on Empty

We are about to take an honest look at one of the most important emotional issues that affect adult children: compulsive-addictive behavior. Before we begin, take a pencil and answer the following questions with either *yes* or *no*, *a* or *b*.

_____ 1. Are you frequently drawn to causes or people that require self-denial or sacrifice?

_____ 2. Do you feel guilty or inadequate when you are unable to help solve problems or help others?

_____ 3. Do you measure your self-worth in terms of what you can do for others?

_____ 4. When you are under positive or negative stress, do you turn to a substance or an activity to relieve it?

_____ 5. Does your need or appetite for the substance or activity increase?

_____ 6. Do you feel ashamed, guilty or defensive about your need to turn to your favorite substance or activity?

_____ 7. Do you begin projects with enthusiasm and find your interest dwindling after a short time?

_____ 8. Are your emotions numb?

_____ 9. Do you think often about food or your weight?

_____ 10. Do you gravitate toward relationships with members of the opposite sex who are abusive?

_____ 11. When someone shows an interest in you, do you tend to smother him or her?

_____ 12. Do you blame yourself when things go wrong?

_____ 13. Do you become angry, frustrated or depressed when people you are trying to help don't change?

_____ 14. Are you a master at "flogging dead horses"?

_____ 15. Do you feel uncomfortable when things are calm?

_____ 16. Do you feel (a) joyful or (b) "burned out"?

_____ 17. Do you spend most of your time rescuing people in one way or another?

_____ 18. Are the people most frequently around you (a) emotionally and spiritually healthy or (b) wounded and hurting?

_____ 19. Do you believe that the well-being of others often hinges on your ability to help them?

_____ 20. Do you feel the need to manage situations and people around you?

_____ 21. Do you often feel deprived, as though others' needs must always come before yours?

_____ 22. Do (did) any of your relatives, including great-grandparents, grandparents, parents, uncles, aunts, cousins, brothers or sisters, have problems with alcohol, drugs (including prescription drugs), workaholism, sexual perversion, or compulsive gambling, spending, eating or dieting?

Score: Compulsive-addictive persons will answer _yes_ and _b_ to these questions. If you answered this way to between one and six of these questions, you are probably beginning to have difficulty with compulsive-addictive behavior; if seven to twelve you are likely inhibited by compulsive-addictive behavior; more than twelve answers and compulsive-addictive behavior is, I would venture, one of your major problems.

Codependency

I saw her slumped alone on the altar weeping, her body heaving as she sobbed until it seemed she could not cry anymore. I bent down to ask her if she wanted someone to pray with her or to pray alone. She raised her face toward me and began to pour out her story. The message at the retreat had touched Kelly on a deep level. She had come asking for guidance and direction, but had gotten answers she had not expected to hear.

For six years Kelly had tried her best to look after her father, a pitiful victim of Alzheimer's disease. Married with three small children, she had bravely consented to letting her father come live in their home after her mother died of cancer. Her father had been afraid of living alone—and frankly Kelly had been concerned about a recurrence of the "drinking problem" he had had when she was growing up. The situation seemed fine until he began to lose his memory.

At first it seemed that he couldn't remember where he was or what he had been doing. The first few symptoms were chalked up to the stress of losing his wife and the onset of old age, but within a few weeks his memory had deteriorated to the point that he couldn't remember names of lifelong friends and relatives or remember who the President was. A visit to the doctor and tests in the hospital revealed that her father had become one of the victims of Alzheimer's disease. The doctor's prognosis indicated

that slowly he would begin to forget everything, his brain crush-
ing memories into fragments and quietly erasing them.

All of Kelly's brothers and sisters agreed that her father should
not go to a nursing home. He had been such a good father and
husband that he deserved to spend the last months or years with
those he loved. He had often said that he never wanted to go to
a nursing home and pled with them in his more lucid moments
not to "put him away." This affirmed Kelly's resolve to do what-
ever was in her power to save her father from the fate he dreaded.

But now her family was beginning to show signs of wear and
tear. Looking after her father had proven to be a task that required 24-hour vigilance. Several times in the middle of the
night the family had awakened to find him gone and appre-
hended him wandering aimlessly through the neighborhood.

At meals he was having difficulty with his table manners and
Kelly's children could no longer bear to watch their grandfather
in such a state. At times he would become angry and frustrated
with himself and blow up, swearing and cursing. Then he would
forget what had happened and lapse back into docile silence,
staring at Kelly and her family as though he didn't know who
they were.

Kelly's husband, Charles, had been patient and understanding
at first, putting himself in Kelly's place, thinking how he would
feel if it were his own father. But now Charles' patience was wearing thin, and he was working longer and longer hours to avoid
coming home. The children would come home from school and
go into their rooms, close their doors and emerge only for dinner.

Several times Kelly had considered placing her dad in a nursing home, but then felt guilty for even considering it. Her brothers and sisters protested the idea vehemently. How could she
abandon him now after all he had done? Occasionally he would
still plead with her not to send him to a nursing home.

As Kelly poured out her pain, I understood what she was going through. She was torn between sacrificing herself for her dad and her responsibility to her immediate family. Kelly's Christianity had played a big part in her decision to look after her dad. After all, Jesus would have done it, wouldn't He? Didn't the Lord expect us to lay down our lives for others? Actually, Kelly's decisions stemmed from more than what she believed to be the leading of the Lord. Kelly had become a victim of an emotional disorder known as codependency.

Codependency is the word used to describe those who sacrifice themselves for others compulsively in order to sustain a sense of self-worth. It is sown and nourished in those who grow up in dysfunctional homes in the presence of glaring need or heart-ache. Codependency takes over the consciences of caring individuals and causes them to become raw and overly sensitive. It is learned as a tradition from parents who also derived their own sense of self-worth from rescuing, managing and caretaking others who had life-controlling problems. Codependency calls more people to helping occupations such as medicine, counseling and ministry than God Himself. It destroys its victims, sucking out of them their joy and fruitfulness and throwing them away on hopeless situations where God has never promised to intervene.

Christians come by this disorder through applying Scriptures unwittingly to their dysfunctional traditions. They often subject themselves to emotionally and physically harmful situations in the name of Christ in order to save the souls of the abusive, but what they are doing is really trying to force the hand of God in places where He does not intend to move. The tradition of martyrdom lies at the root of codependency and pushes its victims to rescue, manage, sacrifice for and mold themselves around the presence of problems such as alcoholism, drug addiction, other forms of abuse, the tragedy of handicapped loved ones and even social causes.

Codependency kills by inducing pessimism, destroying vision, creating stress and condemning its victims to a state of hopelessness. It is at the root of suicide whereby the victim is so tied to circumstances and people beyond himself that he cannot be happy unless outward circumstances permit.

Codependency is a learned reaction to need and a mask for one's own emotional pain. It is a compulsion that alters one's mood and is as addictive as any other substance or activity. Although it seems just the opposite, at its root is a strange form of self-centeredness, an appetite for "helping" that meets a need in the codependent. Because of its selfish origin, it often causes the codependent to deny the presence of real need and causes him to hinder rather than truly help those he believes he is helping. The codependent snatches the role of "savior" from the Lord Jesus Christ and substitutes himself. He becomes the answer-bearer, the problem-solver, the anointed one whose works, sermons, ministry and acts of "kindness" are necessary for rescuing the world. And all the time, the codependent's aching heart is searching for a sense of self-worth.

At the judgment seat of Christ, all of his well-meaning acts of rescue will not profit him because they originated from the good intentions of a wounded soul, not the direction of the Holy Spirit. God wants to get the news to people like Kelly before it's too late that the yoke of Christ is easy and His burden is light.

Kelly had fallen prey to a devious form of deception that was using the facade of the cause of Christ to destroy her family and burn out her emotions. Living with her father's deteriorating condition had caused Kelly to numb herself to emotional pain and in so doing she had numbed herself to joy. Underneath her smile was fomenting a virulent anger, which she readily admitted lashed out at her husband and children and revealed her resentment at the martyrdom she felt God was forcing upon her. She harbored a strange resentment at her father for robbing her family of happiness, her husband for not being more understanding, her children for hiding from their grandfather and at God for doing this to her. She kept holding out hope that her father's condition would improve, that God would heal him, but he only got worse. She felt guilty for holding anger and resentment at her brothers and sisters who never offered to take their father home for even a brief visit and yet expected her to care for him.

What had happened to Kelly happens to all codependents. Without realizing it, she had gotten in over her head. Her compassion had run ahead of wisdom. She had unknowingly brought a major dysfunction into the center of her otherwise healthy family and was expecting them all to join her in rescuing her father—not from death, but from what he needed now, the care of a nursing home. She had forced on them a sacrifice that they did not choose to offer and the resentment was eating away at them all. Kelly was killing those around her with "love."

Dr. Patricia O'Gorman and Philip Oliver-Diaz, who counsel addictive families and who wrote *Breaking the Cycle of Addiction: A Parents' Guide to Raising Healthy Kids*, describe how people become this way:

> Compulsive dependency (co-dependency) is a type of "learned helplessness" that is unconsciously taught to children from birth. Here the child is systematically made dependent on something or someone beyond themselves. Individuals' needs are fulfilled through something or someone else and not directly. This leads to a lack of independent action as the person or the activity on which the dependency is centered becomes the focus of the majority of the individual's emotional energy and time, in lieu of directly taking care of him or herself. . . . This leads to the development of crippling relationships and compulsive behaviors.

Codependency is "people addiction" and like any other addiction eventually becomes all-consuming. Let's look at the difference between what Kelly was doing and the ministry of Jesus.

The Beginning of True Ministry

The difference between codependency to which Kelly fell victim and the ministry of Christ lies in motivation. I think Kelly truly believed that love was the original motivation in helping her father, and perhaps it was, but it degenerated into a sense of obligation that drove her past her limits. Kelly's "ministry" had begun on the wrong foot. It was need-ordained rather than God-ordained.

The ministry of Jesus began at His baptism. As the hungry crowds gathered by the Jordan River and hung on the words of John the Baptist, the first prophet to Israel after centuries of silence, John's gaze became fixed on the lone figure of one man approaching him. The crowd watched as they exchanged a few words. And after John reached out his hand to baptize the man, the heavens opened above them and the voice of God the Father called out: "Thou art My beloved Son, in Thee I am well pleased" (Mark 1:11).

These form the only audible words of ordination that began the ministry of our Lord Jesus Christ. Three elements in this message strengthened Jesus enough to be able to endure the direct confrontation of Satan, forty days of fasting in the wilderness and three years of life-consuming ministry. Those words contained a revelation of: the Fatherhood of God, the affirmation of His love for His Son and the fact that before Jesus ever performed a single miracle, He had already pleased His Father. These are the same words that each Christian needs to hear before he embarks on any work in God's name.

Before I attempt to sacrifice and work, I need a revelation of the Fatherhood of God, the gut-level knowledge that He loves me and that I please Him. It is the message of grace, God's love granted to me not on the basis of my performance, but because He loves me. These words freed Jesus and yet bound Him with one constraint: responding to God's love—not human need. Throughout the remainder of His ministry on earth, Jesus did so many wonderful works on the basis of this revelation that John later wrote, "And there are also many other things which Jesus did, which if they were written in detail, I suppose that even the world itself would not contain the books which were written" (John 21:25).

The revelation of the Fatherhood of God and His unconditional love is the missing ingredient in the lives of adult children. They are compelled to go to great lengths to sacrifice, bestowing all their gifts to feed the poor and giving their bodies to be burned (see 1 Corinthians 13:3) to prove that their love for God is truly genuine and to try to earn His approval, which has already been given. It is the sense that God the Father's unconditional love is missing that causes the adult child to burn himself out.

Are You Burning Out?

In order to illustrate what life would be like in the Church before His Second Coming, Jesus told a parable recorded in Matthew 25:1–12 about ten virgins or bridesmaids who were waiting for the bridegroom to arrive to celebrate His marriage. The bridegroom is Jesus and the virgins are those in the company who are awaiting His return.

Five virgins took lamps and an extra flask of oil, but the other five who were foolish took only the oil in their lamps and no extra oil with them. The bridegroom took so long in coming that they all dozed off to sleep. But sure enough, at midnight the cry came, "Behold the bridegroom! Go out to meet him!" The virgins arose and trimmed their lamps, but the foolish discovered they did not have enough oil. Recognizing that they were running on empty, the foolish said to the wise, "Give us your oil because our lamps are burning out!" But the wise replied, "Go to the dealers and buy some for yourselves." And while they were gone to purchase oil, the bridegroom came. When the foolish returned, the door was shut on the wedding feast.

Let me say first of all that it is no coincidence people all over the Church today are talking about burnout. The term *burnout* has come to mean emotional exhaustion, the emotional numbness that comes from excessive fruitless labor and the disappointment of unrewarded work. And isn't it burnout that causes us to lose heart, fall asleep spiritually and pay no attention to the signs of the times?

The oil in the parable represents the joy that comes from the inner presence of the Holy Spirit. As night fell and the bridegroom did not arrive, all the virgins fell asleep, but some had what others didn't—an extra supply of joy. What codependents lack is joy because the problem persons who have none themselves have drained theirs away and caused their Christian lights to flicker and smolder in the hour of spiritual darkness. As the time of Jesus' coming draws near, the foolish will say to the wise, "Give me your joy!" But the wise who have been healed of codependency will say to the foolish, "No. Go out and get your own from the same place I got mine!"

We cannot allow anyone to drain us so dry that we lose the joy of the Lord and the source of light! Problem persons and situations plead for all we have to give, sucking out of us what they do not want to pay the price to obtain—taking time to fellowship with God. They want to take ours away, and the wise will not give it to them. How can you be sure that you won't become codependent and give away your oil? Knowledge about the origin of compulsive helping, its characteristics and its remedy will help supply you with the extra flask of oil that can't be easily stolen.

When Helping Becomes Compulsive

Like any other addiction, codependency or people addiction supplies a false fuel for your spiritual lamp. It burns for a while but then burns out, leaving you empty and hollow and searching for a new supply. We are living in a compulsive society that has substituted all manner of mood-altering chemicals and activities for the oil of joy of the Holy Spirit.

Addictions replace what the presence and power of the Holy Spirit are to do in a person's life. Paul wrote to the Ephesians: "Be not drunk with wine wherein is excess, but be filled with the Holy Spirit." Alcohol is mentioned specifically in Scripture as the mood-alterer so many turn to, as is *pharmakia*, drugs or "witchcraft" as it is translated in Scripture. We might add food, work, sex, entertainment, gambling, shopping, caffeine and addictive relationships, to name a few.

The word *addiction* in Scripture has two meanings: "beside wine," indicating one who is always found near a bottle; and "to turn to," which portrays the true nature of any addictive substance or process. The addict "turns to" it in time of either positive or negative emotional stress. True addictions consume the body, soul and spirit of the addict and are not controllable through willpower. Rather, they require the gradual renewing of the mind, the moral support of friends and relatives, medical and psychological treatment and help from other trained professionals.

We want to believe that an addiction can be cured by a quick fix such as instant prayer and increased religious fervor, which, ironically, can become an addiction itself. But in an effort to find an easy way out, we fail to find the slow, sure pathway out of bondage, the path of gradual restoration that comes through the one-day-at-a-time learning to change, to trust God and others for help. Let's examine the addictive cycle to see how addictive substances and activities like codependency become the false fuel we rely on to keep us burning.

The Addictive Cycle

My first book, *When Addiction Comes to Church*, exposes the often undiagnosed problem of addiction in the Church body. Hiding behind different masks, many people who claim to have been "totally delivered from drugs and alcohol" continue in compulsive-addictive behavior. In the pulpit and the pew, addiction continues to victimize those who have yet to dig out the roots of this malignant disease.

Addicts in the Church who quit using alcohol and drugs tend to become cross-addicted or addicted to other compulsions that can be equally destructive. Others who attempt to restrain themselves find themselves on a "dry drunk," manifesting all the emotional symptoms of a person actively using alcohol and drugs. Until the Church begins to educate herself concerning the symptoms of addictive behavior, addicts within her borders will remain undiscovered, unhealed and even promoted. This will only generate upheaval in their families and churches and encourage them to fall away out of the shame that comes from compulsively repeating the addictive behavior they feel they should be able to subdue. Part of learning to identify addiction comes from knowing its cycle. I would like to review it here briefly, inserting compulsive rescuing as the mood-alterer.

1) Stress

Every compulsive-addictive person becomes most vulnerable to addiction when he falls under stress. In Kelly's case, the death of her mother and the surrounding circumstances placed the stress in her life that caused her to become anxious and fearful. The fear of abandonment can be stirred in anyone, but Kelly was particularly susceptible after losing her mother to cancer. Without realizing it, she was set up for the next step in the addictive cycle.

2) Contemplation

In the case of a substance addiction, the addict at this point in the addictive cycle begins to experience a mild craving for his mood-alterer. He begins to have thoughts that he needs his addictive substance or process to soothe his emotions. Kelly was in need of comfort herself. But instead of working through the grief process in a healthy way before she made any life-controlling decisions, her sentiment fixed itself on her father's pitiful condition. This was a subconscious way of distracting her from her own pain. As she thought about how much worse her father's grief must have been, she felt that her own pain was eased. She began to consider that helping to solve her father's dilemma was all-important. This set her up for step three.

3) Obsession

During this phase, Kelly became obsessed night and day with worry and pity for her father. She spent her waking moments consulting with her brothers and sisters for advice and convincing her husband and family that they should take her father in. The more she considered it, the more she felt good about herself. Her willingness to sacrifice proved to herself that she was a good

Christian. She began to make arrangements that her father, still in the throes of grief himself, was all too ready to accept as the solution to his emotional pain.

The food addict or alcoholic in this phase begins to become obsessed with the priority of acquiring his addictive substance. Craving has escalated now to the point that the addict thinks of nothing else than how much better he will feel once he has indulged.

4) Compulsivity

During the compulsivity phase of the addictive cycle, the addict turns off reason and becomes mindlessly and uncontrollably propelled toward indulgence in his habit. Unless someone else bodily restrains or interrupts him, the addict will go after his mood-alterer like a zombie.

Kelly ignored during this phase the counsel and questions of several people she respected, including her pastor. She felt they did not understand what she was trying to do when they pointed out that her house was not equipped to handle another person and to suggest that she wait until her grief subsided before making this decision.

5) Indulgence

For six years Kelly had sacrificed, rescued and managed for her father. Like an alcoholic indulging in his drinking binge, Kelly had indulged herself in martyrdom. At first it had satisfied her need to feel worthwhile and useful, and postponed her having to experience her grief. She had simply become too busy to think about it. Then the doctor diagnosed her father's Alzheimer's disease; Kelly now had another more pressing matter to occupy her thoughts. She became consumed with all the actions and thoughts common to all codependents. But little by little her resolve to sacrifice no matter what began to fade into a heavy sense of obligation and duty.

6) Remorse

As other kinds of addicts do after they indulge, Kelly began to feel remorseful. It was her remorse, in fact, that propelled her to the altar the day I met her. When a drug addict awakens to his indulgence or the alcoholic rouses from his drunken stupor, he immediately becomes affected emotionally with pangs of remorse.

During this phase, he often resolves to do better, to make it up to his family members and otherwise atone for the pain he may have caused others. In an attempt to prove that he really can quit on his own, he makes his way to the altar or the confessional to get his "sin" off his chest. Because he has broken his promises to himself, the addict's own conscience is pricked and he turns to methods of reform as a kind of penance. He may weep and make promises to do better and truly believe that he has taken care of his problem, that he has it under control.

Though she felt sorry, Kelly did not see the need for drastic change in her circumstances. She still felt a strange sense of satisfaction at having sacrificed herself, as though it was a means of justifying her existence. She even felt spiritually affirmed as though God were appeased. Codependents, like other addicts, are sometimes able to see that they are in trouble, and even that they are addicted, but do not see the necessary change as imperative.

7) Denial

Thus, one of the symptoms of addiction is the addict's ability to lie to himself, convincing himself and sometimes those around him that he is not truly addicted. After the remorse phase, the craving dissipates. In the absence of craving, it is much easier for the addict to convince himself that all this talk about addiction is too extreme when applied to him. The illusion of control is so strong that he believes he has finally won victory over the matter.

In the past Kelly had sought counseling about her situation, but when others had gently suggested that it was time to put her father's care in better hands, she had felt a slight tinge of guilt—a sense of failure. Determined to try again to do a better job in helping her father by reconsecrating herself to the task of sacrificing for him, she had failed to implement the sound counsel given her.

Kelly, typical of other kinds of addicts, assured me that she didn't need help, that she could manage on her own. Sadly, unwittingly, she set herself up to repeat the addictive cycle. If her father should die, Kelly will only find some other cause or needy person to sacrifice for. A codependent is usually not happy when things are rocking along normally, but is comfortable only in the presence of activity and upheaval that was the norm in their dysfunctional homes. Finding hurting, needy people to console is one way of quenching this appetite for upheaval. In order to sustain her sense of self-worth, Kelly must preoccupy herself with others. Unless she admits she is addicted and gets help, Kelly will eventually burn out.

But doesn't the world really need more people like Kelly who are willing to lay their lives down for others? Isn't it selfish not to? If codependency is wrong, doesn't that imply you should never try to help anybody?

The world needs more people who will obey the Lord Jesus Christ and do as Jesus did; He did the things He saw the Father doing. The world doesn't need more people with Kelly's problem because she has several characteristics that desperately need a healing touch from God. What we need are those motivated not from a sense of obligation and false martyrdom, but from joyful obedience to Jesus Christ. Let's look at the characteristics of codependents that cause them to substitute the "false oil" of caretaking and rescuing in their spiritual lamps.

Addicts are not addicts because they feel like it but because they follow the addictive cycle and possess different *behavioral characteristics*. These include cross-addictions, an inability to accept responsibility for their own problems and sins, impulsiveness in making important decisions, the ability to lie, rebellion against authority, a perfectionistic perspective of themselves and others, anger both concealed and overt, self-pity, and the need to hide their addiction from themselves and others through denial and secretiveness.

Proceeding directly from the tradition of compulsivity, compulsive-addictive behavior begins as a learned response to stress. As the addiction takes over, however, the will is overrun by a force greater than itself and becomes incapable of stopping the whirl of the addictive cycle. If a person is genetically predisposed to chemical dependency, it does not take much exposure to that substance before he becomes "infected" himself. Part of identifying the presence of addiction is taking an honest look at the roots of this tradition in your family.

Exercise

In order to find the roots of addiction and compulsivity in your family, take a sheet of paper and draw your family tree back to your great-grandparents (farther if you know it). Add your brothers and sisters, aunts, uncles and cousins to the branches. Beside each name list any addictions or compulsions you know they possess(ed). If you are undecided, ask yourself the following questions:

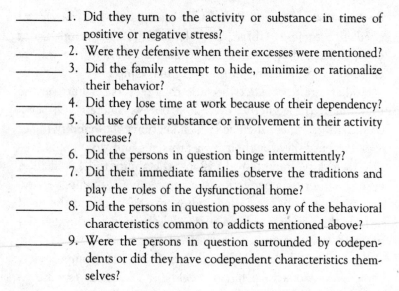

_____ 1. Did they turn to the activity or substance in times of positive or negative stress?

_____ 2. Were they defensive when their excesses were mentioned?

_____ 3. Did the family attempt to hide, minimize or rationalize their behavior?

_____ 4. Did they lose time at work because of their dependency?

_____ 5. Did use of their substance or involvement in their activity increase?

_____ 6. Did the persons in question binge intermittently?

_____ 7. Did their immediate families observe the traditions and play the roles of the dysfunctional home?

_____ 8. Did the persons in question possess any of the behavioral characteristics common to addicts mentioned above?

_____ 9. Were the persons in question surrounded by codependents or did they have codependent characteristics themselves?

When adult children first fill out their family trees looking for signs of compulsivity and addiction, they are sometimes shocked to see that compulsivity and addiction are well-established family traditions for generations. (Not only is using the family tree good for diagnosing the root of compulsive behavior, but also the widespread tendencies toward diseases such as heart disease, cancer, diabetes or other genetic difficulties. How many died of these illnesses? Do you need to alter your health habits to help prevent being victimized?)

If alcoholism is anywhere in your family tree, you should know that using this substance puts you at a much greater risk of developing the disease than others. If national statistics are true, one out of three daughters of alcoholics develops alcoholism and one out of ten sons. Is drinking alcohol worth the risk? Your parents don't have to have been alcoholics for you to develop it; it can show up anywhere in the family tree, randomly selecting its next victim. If members of your immediate family died of heart disease, shouldn't you have a physical, check your blood pressure, know your cholesterol count and change your diet? If your mother and sisters had ovarian cancer, shouldn't you be examined every six months by a gynecologist? How many had the survival mentality, the fear of poverty or other emotional problems? Maybe it's time to break denial and look at facts in black and white!

How many codependents were in your family tree? Codependents possess all the characteristics of other addicts mentioned above. The following list of characteristics more specifically defines their addiction.

1) A Need to Control

The people addict is usually an adult child who has grown up in a situation beyond his/her control. He grew up desperately desiring to be able to exert enough influence to change his unhappy situation. Children of divorced parents often blame themselves for their parents' divorce and fantasize ways of helping them back together. Adult children fear being out of control in any setting and frequently abandon situations and people whom they feel they cannot control.

This need to control manifests itself in the adult codependent's desire to fix situations and people around him. The arrival of difficulty is like dropping the gauntlet. The codependent rises to the occasion by mustering all his managerial powers of analysis and manipulation into making sure the situation turns out right—to his own definition of "right."

When unhealed codependents rise to positions of authority, they frequently go beyond their bounds and attempt to manipulate and control with means such as intimidation and guilt projection. Being highly perfectionistic, they expect and usually obtain compliance from others. If not, they punish by withholding love, approval, money or reward.

2) Anger

Although many codependents do not show it, they are full of unresolved anger and bitterness. Because of the added stress in their lives, which they do not have the grace from God to handle, they expect others to shore them up and share the burden. When others do not, they become angry. Their anger is frequently held behind a smooth, sophisticated mask, but it often erupts over lesser issues or turns inward taking the form of depression. The source of the depression or the fact that he is angry is usually a mystery to the codependent.

3) The Inability to Discipline Themselves

This is a hallmark of compulsives of all kinds. They are either extremely undisciplined, giving in to whims and desires with no ability to control themselves, or they go too far in the other direction, driving themselves for fear that they will once again spin out of control, lose interest or fail to carry out their goals. It is ironic that while they want to control others, they often feel out of control themselves.

4) The Inability to Set Realistic Boundaries

Not only are compulsives unable to achieve balance in self-discipline, but they are notably inept at setting personal boundaries. They are continually invaded by the requests of others and the pressing needs around them. Codependents find it difficult to say no and when they do, they often say no to the wrong things, the things that would help them. Because adult children had abnormal role models and do not know what normal is, they model themselves after their compulsive-addictive parents who do not know when enough is enough.

Christian adult children who are unaware of their codependent tendencies assume more responsibility than God expects of them. They are frequently spread too thin because they haven't been able to determine the true will of God for their lives. As a result, they manifest the next characteristic of codependency.

5) The Inability to Help

The activities of the codependents that are aimed at helping more often than not hurt in the long run or fail to provide anything but momentary relief. All their energy is consumed in keeping problem persons from facing the consequences of their problems, seeking professional help or obtaining better care. Kelly was hurting her father and her family by trying to help in the same way an alcoholic's spouse harms him through denial and helping him cover up the consequences of his addiction.

Christian codependents show a lack of faith in God to be able to handle situations and people without their direct intervention. Part of this is due to the silence they feel from God. *If God isn't listening to me, then how can He respond with the answer to my prayer? I must help solve the problem myself,* he thinks.

6) The Adoption of Causes

The codependent's need to control, coupled with his anger, which must find a vent, propels him to adopt causes for which he can devote himself in some form of martyrdom. The adult child's sense of shame concerning his past internalizes and comes out as the need to "right wrongs." He will take up spiritual-sounding words and phrases and righteous stances. As the cause becomes obsessive, he will stir more internal anger—an emotion that is usually denied by the more spiritual. Causes require compulsivity and workaholism which the adult child is ready to give. The cause cannot live without him or his ministry. All this gradually takes a toll in the emotions and the body, but when the martyr believes Jesus has required it of him, he presses on, not realizing he is headed for trouble.

The following is a brief list of possible causes that all need martyrs: one's own ministry inside the local church or outside its walls, including missionary efforts, crusades, visitation, church growth, preaching on the circuit, volunteering at the church; political causes; social causes, including the homeless, the hungry, the addicted, the codependent, the elderly, victims of natural disasters, the handicapped, the diseased, the mentally ill, the abused and neglected, the poor, pornography, racial and ethnic minorities, immigrants, cleaning up TV, the environment or the church. All of these have proponents who are like giants calling out to the vulnerable codependent, "Send out someone to fight with me!" And the adult child looking for a cause quickly becomes obsessed and enamored of unsheathing his sword. Involvement satisfies his need to control and boosts his sense of self-worth.

Please note that the Bible speaks of a ministry of "helps," a gift of compassion given to many people to help them help others. That gift brings with it peace and joy in serving. To help you distinguish this from codependency look at these five danger signals that point to a codependent involvement with a cause:

1) All of life becomes interpreted by the cause. Spirituality, goodness, worth, all become defined in terms of their relationship to the cause.

2) As a result, all who are not involved in the cause are condemned as unspiritual, not good or less than they should be.

3) As the cause becomes more and more consuming, the code-

pendent loses sight of the fact that God has everything under control. Panic sets in, and fear that the enemy is getting the upper hand drives him to believe that the success of the cause hinges on his involvement in it.

4) Feelings of anger, hostility and resentment surface toward those who do not adopt the cause or who possess opposing views.

5) True devotion to and enjoyment of Jesus Christ and an eager joy to tell others about Him occupies less and less of the codependent's time.

Involvement in causes to the degree mentioned above requires sublimation of one's own fellowship with the Lord Jesus Christ to the cause. No wonder the Church is burning out and the bridesmaids are falling asleep. Everyone is pooped from wearing sandwich boards and passing out campaign literature in parking lots. Involvement in causes when it becomes primary and life-controlling becomes a substitute fuel for the spiritual lamp. When a codependent is unable to effect change, a sense of failure sets in and his self-worth is dealt a severe blow. By the time the codependent realizes that God was not at the root of his obsession, it is too late and the damage to his body, his emotions and his spiritual life is sometimes irreparable.

What does God really want? What is the remedy for the adult child, the codependent who finds himself addicted to sacrificing and helping?

Fresh Oil

The answer for the burned-out adult child is a fresh supply of oil. David observed that the Lord anointed his head with oil the way a shepherd would anoint the heads of his sheep before letting them go out into the bright sun each day: "You anoint my head with oil; my cup runs over." This anointing deterred insects and kept the sheep from suffering a depletion of energy.

In Nehemiah we read, "The joy of the Lord is your strength." Isaiah spoke of "the oil of gladness instead of mourning." David later wrote, "My horn is exalted in the Lord; I have been anointed with fresh oil!" Fresh oil comes to the Christian by moving from the edge of the pasture and drawing closer to Jesus Christ, the Good Shepherd. Here are some benefits.

Time Apart

Codependents have usually neglected their own emotional needs in favor of "helping" others. During the period of restoration, found by drawing close to the Shepherd, the tired sheep will be given a cleansing, food and a "makeover." So often the codependent has been running so hard that he has suppressed anger and bitterness, grief and sadness, and has neglected grateful thanks and praise to God and personal worship. Only when he is quiet and has time to reflect will the roots of his anger be discerned. In Kelly's case, she needed time away to be able to grieve the loss of her mother and the slow death of her father. Emotional discharge is essential in releasing the pent-up stress of negative emotions. Taking time to release negative emotions produces a positive effect in the soul, like letting the pus drain out of an infection. More happens during this period of restoration.

Restoring the Body

In order to contain God's oil of joy, the soul and body must be restored to wholeness. They have the capacity to contain a large deposit, but unless they are in condition, the oil will seep away once again.

Let's face it, once our bodies are dead, we no longer have a ministry. Robert Murray McShayne was a great preacher who, when dying at a young age, said, "God gave me a horse and a message. I've killed the horse. Now I can't carry the message." One symptom of false martyrdom that will go unrewarded on Judgment Day is the exhaustion that comes from being a bad steward of the physical body. We must take care of our bodies; they are the lamps that contain the oil.

Part of taking care of the body means interrupting the codependent cycle—calling all the addictive activities to a screeching halt. The period of quiet restoration may be spent in counseling, in a treatment center or on a vacation, but it must involve separating from the environment that gave rise to the development of the codependency.

Establishing Boundaries

In order to contain the spiritual blessing of fresh oil, the codependent and other addicts must learn to establish boundaries. Like the ancient cities with walls built around them, wise people establish boundaries to protect their privacy. Ministers often allow the congregation to break down their walls and then wonder why they are too burned out to preach on Sunday morning. Jesus often called the disciples to a quiet place to rest awhile. Anyone without a day of rest will burn out quickly and lose his fresh supply of oil.

Nehemiah's ministry was rebuilding the wall of Jerusalem that had been pillaged by the Babylonians. Once he began to build, he received violent opposition from foes without and within. Any codependent will experience the same opposition from people who don't understand why he says no, and from his own conscience that is afraid to say no. But build he must if he plans to contain the gifts and ministries that God entrusts to his stewardship.

Walls must be firm and yet have gates where those permitted to pass may enter in. Walls keep out undesirables but permit passage of those we want to fellowship with, those who will not rip into our stores of oil. Limits simply help us enjoy life.

Being Filled with the Holy Spirit

The Holy Spirit, who dwells inside the Christian, is the source of his oil of gladness. If invited to do so, He will readily offer a fresh supply of joy. We simply ask the Good Shepherd, the Lord Jesus Christ, to fill us with the Holy Spirit's joy and peace.

This property of the Holy Spirit is the theme of the story of the prophet's widow who sought out Elisha's help to repay her creditors. Elisha told her to take the only thing she had left in the house, which was a jar of oil, to collect as many empty vessels as she could from her neighbors and to begin pouring the oil in her jar into the empty containers. As she poured into first one and then another, she was amazed that the oil kept coming. In fact, she ran out of vessels before she ran out of oil. The characteristic of the Holy Spirit to replenish emptiness with a never-ending supply is clearly seen here. When God's blessing is on the work, the one ministering will never run out. Obedience to the Lord is the key.

Love

The false fuel of codependency is a substitute for real love. While real love may lay its life down for another, it does so joyfully.

I mentioned earlier how, for many years, our inner-city church ministered to helpless people with a variety of problems from poverty to mental illness. The run-down building in which we met and the "cause" we espoused attracted codependents like flies to flypaper! Many of us burned ourselves out with very little fruit. Without realizing how many of our number were susceptible to codependency, we gave and gave until giving became a drudge.

After realizing the truth about addiction and codependency, we began to search our motives for all the sacrificing we had been doing. By this time our church had moved to the small town outside of Pittsburgh which, as I have already shared, saw some codependents lose their cause and leave the church. Determined not to be drawn by need alone, we submitted to the Lord and began to wait. It was difficult because adult children become easily upset when there is no flurry of activity, no crisis or cause.

Then in 1989 we heard about the plight of Christian refugees coming out of the Soviet Union and desiring to be repatriated in the free world. Something different touched our hearts as we scanned their photographs in magazines, their faces lit with expectation. Through prayer and preparation we decided to invite one of these families to be a part of our church. Before, when we had embarked on projects in the city, a sense of duty and obligation had driven us forward. Finances usually dripped and trickled but never flowed, even though many people gave all they could to the work at hand.

But this time things were different. When we had committed ourselves to do it, we instantly felt ourselves flowing in the rushing river of God's will. The people who worked on the project were constantly taken aback by the hundreds of tiny miracles and fast answers to prayer that went into the preparation.

Vitali and Maria Dorosh and eleven children arrived on September 30, 1989. Did we have enough oil for thirteen vessels and enough food for thirteen stomachs? God faithfully supplied an abundance. There was such an outpouring of love from the community and from the church that as the months have gone by Vitali and Maria and the children have made a firm, loving commitment to our community and to the church.

Their customs were so different from ours that shortly after their arrival, they began to experience what all immigrants experience: culture shock. Vitali and Maria were shocked that American Christian women wore makeup and earrings and pants and that we clapped our hands during the services. Disturbed by this, Vitali went home from church and began to pray.

Later, in his broken English, he stood and told the church his battle and what God had said to him. It has been the commitment to love that has kept Vitali and his family a part of us even as other Soviet immigrants are abandoning their American churches because of the strangeness of customs and differences in doctrine. Vitali said, "I prayed about zis and God say to me, only love—for in the sky [heaven], we all wear the same clothes." Rather than pouring our love into empty containers as we had for so many years, at the instruction of the Lord to pour, we poured, and we see no shortage of oil.

God is looking for balance. There are those who would take the truth about codependency to the other extreme and use it as an excuse not to give at all or do anything unpleasant unless the mood strikes them. But the one who never gives will find himself as empty as the one who gives too much to the wrong cause. The one who finds the balance of the Lord will be able to walk the narrow road between codependency and coldheartedness in the blessing of the Lord.

In the next chapter, we will look at what it takes to remove the pain from the memories that haunt our lives. Learning to let go of emotional pain is for many adult children the most difficult but the most rewarding step toward emotional healing.

13
Taking the Pain Out of Memories

In a nursing home outside Pittsburgh lives a 98-year-old woman named Stella who loves to play bingo and talk about her children. When Nancy, one of the staff members of our church, took a part-time job at this nursing home and began visiting Stella, she felt that the Lord was drawing her to each visit. Stella's eyes never twinkled and the lines on her face seemed to be carved out of years of bitterness. As Nancy visited her, the story unfolded—the loss of two husbands, illness and the normal vicissitudes of life. But Stella's source of resentment went back more than ninety years to her childhood.

Her mother was a stern Christian. Scrubbed and pressed into their best clothes, Stella and her siblings survived each church service with the eager anticipation of leaving. Her mother talked about God at home and at church, but her life bore little resemblance to the love talked about in the Scriptures. Stella's mother was physically abusive, depriving her children of affection and love and substituting a form of sterile dogmatism in its place. It was Stella's father who never went to church who showed them love.

Stella mentioned this absence of love and the contrast between her parents in every conversation with Nancy and refused stubbornly to attend the nursing home church services. "I want nothing to do with God or church. My mother took us to church every Sunday and she was as mean as a snake. I want nothing to do with a God like that!" she would flare with eyes blazing. Stella's daughter, who visited her mother often, attended church herself, but told Nancy, "You'll never get her to go. We've tried for years."

Nancy refused to give up, however, and one day, remarkably, Stella accepted Jesus Christ and released her painful memories to His soothing grace.

Childhood memories are the ones that are first written on the impressionable fibers of our minds. The blessing or curse our childhood was remains with us always and, like the foundation of a building, determines how much the body, mind and spirit can stand. It affects how we view the world around us and what we expect life to hold. The childhood lives through the power of memories. Time marches on, but childhood memories survive until the grave.

Learning to Grieve

Stella's painful memories are like those of other adult children who are haunted and driven by the recollection of past hurts, deliberate and accidental, the omissions of love, unfulfilled promises and frightening moments when the prospect of abandonment or harm was real or imagined. The human emotions can withstand only so much before they must be discharged. If healthy discharge of emotions is not forthcoming, the griefs and sorrows are swallowed into the cavern of the soul and torment the victim with stress-related illnesses and unhappy feelings. When the conscious mind is focused on a memory, the pain is often as real as it was when the event occurred. Sometimes the mind twists the memory into a lie, either exaggerating its misery or minimizing its effect. Unless those events are grieved and the negative emotions associated with them vented, the pressure of the thought builds up in the soul and presses for release. Recollection only brings more pain, never the needed discharge.

How does a person grieve and why?

Those who see grieving every day have learned that all who experience loss must pass through its dark hallways back into the sunshine of emotional health. The adult child is often locked in one of the stages of grief and unable to bring the painful memories of the past to resolution. An understanding of the normal grief process will help the adult child release his grief and move on to resolution.

Shock

The first of these stages of grief is shock, which produces physical symptoms such as a knot in the stomach, a tightened throat, the feeling of being startled into a cold reality you don't want to face. Your emotions can go numb as you fumble for your chair or hold onto a stable object because of weakness. Shock allows you to function instinctively, passing through the motions of living as you adjust to a terrible truth. This is not real grief, only its prelude.

Adult children were rarely free from the experience of shock as children. In fact, addiction counselor Wayne Kritsberg, author of *Adult Children of Alcoholics Syndrome*, has identified the source of the adult child's numb emotions as "chronic shock syndrome." The daily routine of hearing parents fighting or of being threatened with beatings and violence created repeated exposure to emotional shock and caused the child to be locked in this overture to grief. Thus, the adult child attempts to cope with life and relationships with the numb emotions that accompany shock, which should have been only a temporary measure.

Jesse, a friend and Southern Baptist pastor's wife, shared with me the daily fear of seeing her alcoholic father storm into a rage, grab his gun and threaten to shoot the members of the family. "I would sit outside in the meadow waiting for the sound of the gun to go off, always wondering if this would be the day he would carry out his threat." If the grief over such incidents is not experienced and resolved, the adult child in toxic shock will move into denial.

Denial

During denial, the grieving becomes sublimated further as the bereaved person continues to behave as though the tragedy never occurred—as if, for instance, the loved one is still alive. Until the loss is acknowledged, the survivor will continue to speak of his lost loved one as though he were alive or continue to include him in his plans. The fact that he is gone and never coming back is too harsh to handle, so the bereaved insists that there is some mistake, that the tragedy never occurred. Denial can last for moments or years and as long as it lasts, it prolongs moving into the period of deepest emotional suffering.

Sometimes the fear of discharging emotion can keep the adult child locked in denial. Adult children whose emotional states are numb are locked in denial about the extent of their pain and the fact that loss ever occurred. And yet, their inability to feel joy or to be able to recall childhood memories tells the tale.

Anger

When denial finally breaks down, the bereaved person is usually unable to understand why he feels angry. He may be angry at God for not intervening, angry at loved ones for making simple choices that affected the outcome of the tragedy or angry at himself. The anger that adult children harbor is sometimes directed at the problem person for creating dysfunction, at parents for abuse or neglect, at siblings for their irresponsibilities and at others outside the family for not understanding.

Christians deny anger even more than they deny sin. To be angry is to have lost control, to have failed—something that the perfectionistic adult child fears admitting. But feeling angry is the normal reaction to mistreatment, whether or not the abuse was intentional. Acknowledging anger and being able to express it is essential to the resolution of grief.

For years I was ashamed at feeling angry with God when my father died at age 58. He was too young to die, especially in the face of my prayers for his healing. I was so angry with God that I told Him I didn't love Him anymore and that I wouldn't serve Him because He didn't answer me. I can remember crying bitterly on my pillow and feeling betrayed by the Almighty. But dying is a part of living and we can't escape that portion of the curse unless we are in the last generation before Christ's coming.

Anger must find an appropriate release whether through screaming, beating a pillow or describing your feelings to someone else. It is a natural emotion and when Christians try to swallow and deny it, they render themselves sick with the unresolved grief that accompanies it. If anger is not released immediately, suppressed anger can control the emotions and render them numb and dysfunctional. Inappropriate releases of anger erupt on innocent parties who do not understand the violent outburst and whose emotions can become scarred by it. Thinking back on it now, releasing my anger toward God was the healthiest thing I could have done—the thing He probably wanted me to do. I didn't understand that I was moving through anger toward resolution of my grief. I got over being angry with God, and apparently He got over it, too.

Guilt

Not far behind anger is usually guilt, the voice that cries, "If only I hadn't," or, "If only we had." It is normal to feel that you should have made different choices that would have affected the outcome of the tragic event. In her booklet "Healing Grief," Amy Hillyard Jensen describes the feelings of a young mother who neglected to make sure the back doors of her car were locked. Even though her older children had declared that the doors were locked, one door flew open and one small child fell out and was killed. Her feelings of guilt were overwhelming until she came to this realization: "I asked myself, if I had my child back, could I promise that I would never make another mistake? I knew I could not make that promise."

Because we are human, we will make choices and others will make choices that affect the outcome of events. Two cars collide at an intersection because of the split-second timing of choices made that day. If you had the day to relive, you could not guarantee that the choices you made would not be made again and that the outcome would be any different. When tragic choices are made, the frail human being can only cast himself on the redemptive power of Jesus Christ who can turn the tragedy into our highest good.

The adult child cannot relive the events under which he was victimized, the events that robbed him of the pleasant memories that should belong to every child. Pain is a part of living, and I have often wondered if everyone doesn't learn the same lessons of life through experiencing a variety of events. While one person learns about pain by growing up with an abusive parent, another grows up as an orphan. Who can say which is to be preferred? They are both the results of the Adamic curse. Even children who grow up in seemingly happy homes experience other forms of deprivation and loss. My mother told me never to wish that I was in another person's place. Not only would I experience their advantages, but also their share of pain and grief. As we look at the lives of others, I don't think we want to borrow their troubles. God can give us the grace to live through our own.

Despair

Guilt usually gives way to one of the deepest stages of grief, which is despair. After my father died the Saturday after Thanksgiving, we had to live through four weeks of Christmas preparation. Who could even think of Christmas when Pop wouldn't be there to open his gifts, some of which were already bought for him? An overwhelming sense of despair weighed upon me when at times I felt as though I didn't want to live, either. If depression is anger turned inward, it is easy to understand the magnitude of the depression common to the grieving. Weeks after the funeral, it still was hard to carry out even the small details of living. But like the other stages of grief, this one passed also. When you are walking through a house and the power goes out, it's always best to keep walking toward the door. That's what it felt like to walk through that stage of grief. One foot in front of another. One day at a time. And little by little, the dawn started to come.

Some people get stuck in the stage of depression following a tragedy. Professional counselors see people often who after several months or years are still in the throes of depression. Adult children whose unreleased emotions are locked in a tunnel of despair are only going through the motions of living. I believe that many of them are living in a state of chronic depression and have been since childhood because they were never given the prescription for resolving their grief or knew that they were even grieving. They were unable to use the organ of their emotions effectively to release the intense internal emotional pressure.

One woman in her sixties named Mabel approached me after a talk I gave one day. Mabel grew up the child of an alcoholic. Despite her vow never to marry an alcoholic, she did.

In her 45 years of marriage she had lived with the same horror she had grown up with. As her resentment of her husband's drinking grew, she shut down her emotional response toward him. She refused to show him any affection or love. Mabel never instituted divorce proceedings because she felt that wouldn't be Christian. But in her heart Mabel had been divorced for forty years.

Now she felt no emotion about anything at all and hadn't for years—no love for anyone, no joy, no grief. Reaching out for my hand, she was hoping that I could offer a prayer for instant relief. While prayer was a beginning, Mabel will be healed only if she allows the grieving process to continue.

Resolution

The resolution of grief comes only as we allow ourselves to grieve, to weep, to feel sad. Adult children are often frightened of releasing emotions, fearing that once they begin to cry they may not be able to stop. They fear expressing anger because they might fly into an uncontrollable rage. This is again a manifestation of the perfectionistic, all-or-nothing perspective that colors every aspect of their lives. The truth is that human emotions will remain dysfunctional like atrophied limbs unless they are exercised with laughter, exhilaration, sadness, grief and despair. Paul experienced times when he said, "We were burdened excessively, beyond our strength, so that we despaired even of life" (2 Corinthians 1:8). This does not sound like a man afraid to experience his emotions!

A close study of the life of Christ reveals that Jesus experienced every human emotion, including laughter and exuberant joy. Bill informs me that the Greek New Testament expresses Jesus' exuberance when He realized that God had given the mysteries of the Kingdom to babes and hidden them from the wise. The word for *rejoice* in that passage means "to be exuberant with great leaping about." He also became angry with the scribes and Pharisees and even called them names. And He performed one of the most astounding miracles of His earthly ministry, raising Lazarus from the dead, with tears of grief still coursing down His cheeks.

If Jesus could experience the depth of every human emotion and still maintain His holiness and position of authority, then the perfect person is one who can live life and exercise his emotions, too. It is through—not apart from—the emotions that we are able to touch God. In order for them to be healed, they must be exercised, like learning to walk again. You may stumble and fall, but since you no longer have to be a perfectionist, you can make a mistake and get over it. But in order to be healed and resolve your grief, you must admit it and experience it in order to move into resolution.

Besides crying and expressing anger, another way of releasing painful memories is by talking with understanding people about your pain. Many Christians are seeing the need to submit to counseling regarding the emotional issues that continue to bind them in chains of regret. Talking with professionals who can perceive the patterns of the problems that affect you can provide the insight you need. Counselors are able to validate the painful experiences of childhood and help you recognize that although others may have different details to tell, your experiences are common to all dysfunctional families. Several members of our congregation have been greatly helped by good professional Christian counselors. Others find help talking through their experiences in support groups or with friends who understand the pain of a dysfunctional childhood. Regardless of what road you believe is for you, talking with an understanding person about the events and how you felt about those events releases the emotional stress associated with the memories.

I have made three visits in my life to the Grand Canyon. Before I ever saw it the first time I wondered, as we were driving there, if a bridge would cross it as with other great chasms of the world. Someone said, "You haven't seen the *Grand* Canyon!" Indeed, she was right. The massive chasm that caused the early Spanish explorers to fall to the ground and worship God looks like a place where God must have stepped onto the earth. It is ten miles across, over a mile deep and more than two hundred miles long. The only way to traverse it is down the trail, through the bottom, across the raging Colorado River and up the other side, a journey of several days.

No one has ever built a bridge—or wanted to. Walking across a bridge might get us to the other side quicker, but we would miss the point of the Grand Canyon. We shouldn't run across it. Everyone needs to stand there, see his own finiteness and realize there is only one way to the other side: through its depths.

Likewise, there is no help in making bridges over gaps that can be traversed only with the depth of human emotions. The soul is the organ that enables us to experience life, to study its depths and rise to new heights again at the other side, with a clearer understanding of God—and more sympathy for the plights that befall others. When grief joins your repertoire of experiences, it changes you. You don't emerge as the same person you were before.

Rising out of grief sometimes takes determination. Some stay on the canyon's floor afraid to walk out and thus rob themselves of discovering the faithfulness of God and the satisfaction of having passed through and survived. The emotions sometimes need the exercise obtained only from experience. Am I glad my father died? No. I never will be. But I am glad I know what it is to grieve and how God can bring me out again.

Letting your emotions out is the only way to healing and resolution. I wonder if today you wouldn't agree to let God take you through the steps of grief over your childhood experiences, to relieve the painful memories you fear to look at, those that still bring pain when you think of them. You need that canyon experience. God will not push you in; you must trust Him enough to walk in with Him. Why don't you find a private place to let out your rage, to weep at your sense of shame and find out that your almighty Father is right there with you, understanding and saying, "It's all right, go ahead and cry."

Let's look now at the final stage in the process of resolving grief. Because this next step is so important, I want to devote a chapter to it.

14
The Giant Step of Forgiveness

There is something wrong with much Christian teaching about forgiveness. I myself taught in the past, as I have mentioned, that it was wrong to feel anger, a lack of faith to shed tears and not necessary to admit shame. During the years I taught that way, my emotions were numb and I practiced all the dysfunctional roles and traditions of a person whose soul didn't function properly. I was emotionally unhealthy and didn't even realize it. And I was full of anger and bitterness and unreleased rage. The pressures of childhood memories, of being a pastor's wife, of being misunderstood, abandoned and rejected usually by other Christians built up behind my hardened heart like flood pressure behind a dam.

I knew forgiveness was important and tried mentally to go through the exercise of forgiveness, but was dismayed to find that recollections of people who had hurt me still stirred feelings of anger and resentment. Hadn't I chosen to forgive them? Yes, I had. But without allowing myself to exercise my emotions, grief over the experiences still remained.

Too often the dysfunctional try to "jump the canyon" by making a mental decision to forgive and yet continue to deny that they have been hurt or offended. To admit their feelings would be to admit that they are imperfect. Some try to hide shameful experiences such as sexual abuse because they are afraid to experience the emotions that accompanied the experience so long ago. Plus, to admit it may mean not only grief but facing the need to leave home or take legal action or seek help. While society should perhaps not forgive without legal action for crimes like incest and child abuse, the victim must descend the canyon of grief and come to resolution.

Resolution of grief is complete only when forgiveness takes place. Forgiveness is necessary, like burying a dead body. Burying memories when they are still alive is wrong, but once grief has occurred and resolution has eased its pain, there comes a day when it needs to be buried—not in the dark recesses of the soul, but under the blood of Jesus Christ. Many people claim to have buried their memories "under the blood," but they have really put them in their wounded souls and continue with dysfunction in their lives. Dysfunction is an evidence of unresolved grief. These hurting people are afraid to look at the memories. They dread the emotions the memories still stir and the implication of facing them. This is denial and sham and unhealthy Christian living. Burying memories alive means bypassing grief and forgiveness, and leaving the memories to cry out from the grave and haunt them.

Jesus' brand of forgiveness was different from the sterile, emotionless rite of expiation proclaimed by the religious of His day. Jesus' forgiveness included forgiving from the heart. This meant an emotional change that permeated the whole attitude toward the person who had done the hurtful thing. But how is this possible? How is it possible to forgive a father's incest, or a mother's harsh physical abuse?

Is there a secret to making forgiveness real? We know that expressing the grief is crucial. Once that is accomplished, what comes next?

The Grace to Forgive

Jesus promised that "all things are possible to him who believes." When Jesus Christ entered history, the day dawned in which nothing shall be impossible with God—including forgiveness in our hearts. Adult children need what every person needs—the supernatural grace given only by God to let go of offenses. He will lead us through acknowledging them, breaking denial over the fact that they happened, moving on through grief and only then committing to forgive. When this is accomplished, He will help us allow ourselves to forget.

One of the most tragic stories of child abuse I have ever read was the book *Abused But Chosen* by Elsie Isensee Hill.

The details of severe mental and physical torment from her mother while her father was away are heartbreaking. I need not relay them here, but one quote from Elsie reveals the depths of her pain:

After one stinging lecture from her father who had been told that Elsie was guilty of an infraction she didn't commit, she wrote, "I dug my fingernails into my arms in an effort to stifle the hurt as I cried out, 'Oh, God, I wish I could die. Oh, God, I wish I were dead. . . .' "

When her father finally discovered the extreme cruelty to which she was subjected in his absence, he made immediate arrangements for her to leave home. This validation of her pain by her father comforted her briefly but she never received that which she had always longed for, a tiny drop of parental approval. When I read her story, my arms ached to hold my own children and heap upon them the affection she never received. But Elsie's story has a happy ending that demonstrates the power of forgiveness.

Shortly after leaving home, she attended a church service with friends. After a guest minister preached about the fires of hell, the pastor stood up and emphasized the loving arms of almighty God outstretched to hold the repentant sinner. Elsie began to weep. She ran to the altar into the arms of almighty God and sobbed on the altar tears of relief and gratitude at finally finding Someone who would love her unconditionally. She stood to give a few words of testimony, but immediately fell on the altar again, sobbing over the wondrous idea that God loved and accepted her. This experience began a lifetime of restoration by her heavenly Father.

Immediately upon receiving the Lord Jesus Christ, a supernatural desire—which could only have come from God—came into her heart: to tell her mother about the love and forgiveness of God. She embarked on a years-long venture of prayer and inner healing that ended at the bedside of her mother who lay dying of cancer. Only a few days before her mother's death, Elsie, the child her mother had so despised and rejected, was the one who led her to the loving arms of Jesus Christ and the forgiveness of God the Father. And three times before her mother's death, Elsie finally heard her say, "I love you."

Could three brief sentences of validation wash away years of emotional pain? No, they could not. This was where the supernatural grace of God stepped in. Only God can heal the absence of human love. Regardless of the form of our pain, it is only the factor of God's grace that makes the equation come out balanced. Beside mountains of suffering stands the power of God's grace to heal, to forgive and to love.

Forgiving means giving away grace. Until you have experienced it yourself, you don't have it to give. But once you ask for the storehouse of God's grace to open to you, you see a limitless supply of supernatural grace available to pour out on those who don't deserve it either. Sometimes it's hard to pick it up and give it away. In fact, giving it away freely without expecting apologies or amends is impossible without God. When you feel inadequate to give grace, ask for God's power to forgive.

My father, who experienced such emotional pain himself, left a legacy for me inscribed on the flyleaf of his Bible. Whether it was a small snatch from one of our pastor's sermons or something he read in an inspirational magazine, I don't know. It reads: "The one who refuses to forgive, destroys the bridge over which he himself must cross." There are gaps in our perfection, canyons of human disappointment, and in spite of our tries to be perfect, we will create ditches and valleys of despair in others' lives. How can we repair the damage and restore what was stolen? We can't. But when Jesus died, He laid His own body across the valley we created by our sin and failure and gave us a pathway to healing, the ability to receive forgiveness and the power to give it. It is not in man's emotional repertoire to forgive some of the most heinous crimes of deliberate human hatred, but fortunately it is in God's. When we need it, it's there. Grace for the moment, grace for the task, grace when you need it, grace when you ask.

So often I have tried to exert my human emotional power and jump across the canyon created by my or someone else's sin. But I can only sink into the arms of Jesus and ask Him for the power to forgive when I can't muster the power on my own. I think He wants us to face situations impossible for our human effort in order to demonstrate the power of His grace.

The Power of Grace

Forgiveness is giving away grace freely, admitting offense but deciding not to chalk it up on your list of grievances. It is giving the other a break, because one day you will need it, too. Forgiveness holds the power to break the curse of your dysfunctional home, its wounds and emotional scars for you and your inheritance forever. And it is often ignored in solutions offered by secular counselors. It is the privilege of the redeemed and has the power to change not only you but the one you forgive.

Stephen was the first person to be martyred for his belief in the Lord Jesus Christ. This man who was anointed to preach with conviction and do signs and wonders was dragged before the Jews and stoned for heresy. As those who stoned him laid their coats at the feet of Saul of Tarsus, Stephen raised his eyes upward and saw a vision of Jesus standing at the right hand of God ready to receive him. "Lord Jesus, receive my spirit—and do not charge them with this sin," he cried with his last breath.

Stephen's forgiveness broke the power of the curse of generations from Saul who later wrote that he was "a Hebrew of Hebrews . . . a Pharisee . . . a persecutor of the church" (Philippians 3:5–6). Saul had inherited the curse of merciless religious zeal and its perfectionism and was doomed for destruction. But Stephen prayed, the curse was broken and the forgiveness from that one brief Christlike prayer has flowed like ripples in a pool throughout the centuries and still blesses the Church today through the ministry of the apostle Paul. Suppose Stephen had not forgiven Saul when he was still a sinner. What if he had withheld grace? I wonder if we realize how important it is to show others the grace shown us.

This power of grace was brought home to me when I learned how my friend Barb was led on a journey to inner healing that included facing a grudge she had held against her sister-in-law for more than 35 years. Her husband's sister had opposed their marriage and had treated her coolly ever since. But as Barb realized she held anger and bitterness toward her sister-in-law and that its roots had wrapped themselves around her own emotions, she wanted to forgive.

"I couldn't forgive all those years of resentment and rejection until the Lord helped me. He gave me the supernatural ability to forgive from my heart and mean it when I asked His forgiveness and determined to give it away."

Part of Barb's resolution came in writing a letter to her sister-in-law, which she never mailed. In the letter she described her feelings toward her. As she wrote, she let the anger and bitterness surface, admitting not only how she felt, but her remorse over having held it so long. Then she asked her sister-in-law's forgiveness. She resolved her grief and only then buried the memory now dead in its power to affect her. She dated the letter and placed it in a drawer.

Several months later she was at a family reunion where she saw her sister-in-law on the other side of the room. She stepped out gingerly to initiate her first contact with her in years. But as she drew closer, she could tell that something had happened to her sister-in-law. Instead of the sour attitude and the bitter expression to which she was accustomed, her sister-in-law's face was full of peace and delight. She seemed as happy to see Barb as Barb was to see her. Then she found out why.

Several months before the reunion, Barb's sister-in-law had accepted Jesus Christ and had experienced a life change. She was anxious to make amends with Barb as well. "When did you receive Christ?" Barb asked. Her sister-in-law told her the date. When Barb got home, she went to the drawer and took out the letter. Written at the top was the same date that her sister-in-law had accepted Christ.

Was it possible that Barb's decision to give grace away to her sister-in-law held the key to her salvation? When Jesus breathed on the disciples in the Upper Room after His resurrection, He said, "If you forgive the sins of any, their sins have been forgiven them; if you retain the sins of any, they have been retained" (John 20:23). For 35 years Barb had retained the sins of her sister-in-law in her wounded soul, but the day she forgave them, Jesus released both women from the power of sin.

After you have grieved over the childhood memories and the heartaches begin to fade, it is time to forgive those whose sins and shortcomings have caused your pain. The first step is to ask God, your heavenly Father, to give you the grace to forgive from the heart. As His child, you have His divine nature within you, and it is within your ability to release the person by your willingness to dispense grace. Perhaps you need to repent from holding ill will and bitterness in your own heart. After you have asked, there is something else you can do.

Jesus taught His disciples, "Bless them that curse you, do good to them that hate you, and pray for them which despitefully use you, and persecute you." Why? "That ye may be the children of your Father which is in heaven" (Matthew 5:44–45, KJV). Begin to bless verbally the parents who have hurt you and have passed on a curse to you. Turn away their harshness with kindness instead. As you walk the pathway to emotional healing, this will become easier.

Not only should you bless them, but begin to pray for them. In the beginning this may be difficult. Many will say, "I have prayed for years for my parents' salvation but to no avail." Try placing yourself in their stead and begin to pray to the Father the way you know they need to pray from their perspective. Perhaps they were themselves abused as children and knew no other way of treating you. Pray intercessory prayers explaining to God the feelings they must have felt and feel now, the sense of shame, the fear of abandonment, the terror of living outside the Good Shepherd's fold. Praying like this causes you to touch the heart of God as Stephen did and also gives you an insight into what they must be feeling, locked in the prisons of their dysfunctional emotions.

Will everyone I forgive and pray for change? No. But your forgiveness will still release you from the prison of your dysfunctional emotions, bring increased blessing into your own life and take the pain out of memories.

Sometimes you need to release forgiveness to those who are dead. While it cannot change them now, I believe it can change you and is a key to breaking the curse from your life and the lives of your children. Passing on bitter memories to your children serves only to perpetuate the curse, but acknowledging the hurt, experiencing the pain of memories long ago buried alive and laying them to final rest under the blood of Jesus Christ works a miracle in your emotions. It restores your power to forget. Memories that have been buried alive keep resurfacing with pain, but once they have been laid to rest, you will be amazed to find that you can recall them without the pain.

Experiencing grief and forgiveness is not a one-time event. You may be surprised that throughout your life from this moment painful thoughts will rise up over incidents you are committed to forgiving. Weep as often as it takes to release the emotions. Do not allow your pride to put the memory in its box and bury it alive in the recesses of your soul. Little by little you are moving toward complete emotional healing. Remind yourself that it is a process, not a single event.

Before we lay to rest the matter of painful memories, take the following quiz to see how you are doing in forgiving those who have cursed you.

Do You Need to Forgive Someone?

_____ 1. Are all or most of your thoughts about this person negative?

_____ 2. Do you avoid seeing him or talking to him if possible?

_____ 3. Do you feel a flicker of anger, a sense of heartache or even experience rage when he comes to mind?

_____ 4. Do you feel nothing at all for him, even though the relationship is close to you?

_____ 5. Has this person offended you?

_____ 6. Are you able to pray blessings on this person and feel warmth in your heart toward him?

_____ 7. Do you find yourself justifying your dislike for this person with spiritual-sounding words and phrases such as *discernment*?

_____ 8. Do you usually speak negatively about him to others?

_____ 9. Would you want to forgive him if he asked you to right now?

_____ 10. Would you rejoice or feel glad if this person were given an advantage you wanted to have?

Score: If you are having difficulty forgiving the person in question, you will answer this way: *yes* to numbers 1, 2, 3, 4, 5, 7, 8 and *no* to 6, 9, 10.

*   *   *

If you still need work in this area, don't despair. Keep at it and God will help your heart to change.

15
Inheriting the Blessing

By the end of their forty-year wilderness experience, Moses had brought the children of Israel to the border of the land that God had always chosen for them. It would be a pleasant place, a lovely setting for generations of pleasant memories to come, and if they would follow through on their commitment to listen to God and obey Him, they would take up residence there and it would become their very own.

The people to whom Moses was now speaking were the children of the slaves who had served the Pharaoh. Their fathers had never been able to forget the abuses of their past. They had been unable to trust God enough to enter the land. The wilderness, rather than proving their faithfulness, proved instead that the power of painful memories can keep us from God's best. It took forty years for attitudes to fade, for perspectives to change and for a new generation that couldn't remember the pain of Egypt to be able to walk with confidence in God and take the land.

Moses stood to speak to the crowd and in his last words to the children of those who had been "addicted" to Egypt, he said, "I have set before you life and death, the blessing and the curse." Which one they experienced would be determined by their own choice to love God, to walk in His ways and keep His commandments. "So choose life in order that you may live, you and your descendants . . . that you may live in the land which the Lord swore to your fathers, to Abraham, Isaac, and Jacob" (Deuteronomy 30:19–20).

God offers the same choice to adult children who have emerged from the bondage of dysfunctional living. As Jeremiah and Ezekiel echoed centuries later, "If a son observes all the evil which his father commits and in observing does not do likewise," he shall be blessed and not cursed. Choosing blessing does not simply mean choosing the results of the blessing. Rather, it means choosing to walk the pathway to that blessing every day of your life.

Joshua, Israel's new leader after Moses, took up the sword and led the nation of adult children into the Promised Land of blessing. In the first chapter of Joshua, we read that the Lord spoke to these adult children and addressed every emotional issue to affect each adult child ever to live on the earth. To a nation of people who would have difficulty knowing what normal was, the Lord told them to meditate on His Law day and night so that they might prosper and have good success. To a generation that had inherited the fear of abandonment, God said again and again, "I will not leave you nor forsake you, for the Lord, your God, is with you wherever you go." To a fearful, timid people unsure of themselves and insecure, He said repeatedly, "Be strong and courageous; do not be afraid or dismayed." The Almighty had taken up this nation of orphans and completely committed Himself, His love and His miraculous power to their cause. The success of Israel would depend on how much they believed and trusted Him.

Every adult child coming out of the womb of tragic experiences must develop a theology, a knowledge of God, based not on the reactions of their wounded souls, but on the revelation of the Lord Jesus Christ in the Scriptures and through the power of the Holy Spirit. Everyone has a theology, a set of beliefs about God that determines the limits of his experiences. When Jesus said, "According to your faith be it unto you," He meant that our experiences are affected positively or negatively not only by God's will, but by our faith, our understanding of who He is. Your portion of "the land" will only be as big and as clear as your concept of God.

Recently, a crowd of Muslims thronged toward their holy city of Mecca on a pilgrimage, a journey that each faithful Muslim desires to make at least once in his life. As the crowd pressed its way through the underground tunnel that feeds into the city—a tunnel closed to unbelievers—the power suddenly went out and shut off the tunnel's lights. A terrible panic swept through the crowd of once-eager worshipers. They began to search frantically for the opening to the tunnel. A stampede ensued and by the time power was restored, more than 1,500 men, women and children had been crushed to death under the feet of their fellow believers.

When several Muslim spokesmen and spectators were interviewed, each one stated emphatically, "This was the will of Allah." One man said that if they had been in any other place, they would have died at that moment anyway. This view of God imprisons its advocates in a spiritual tunnel of death. But, unfortunately, so does the theology of many Christians.

Too often our theology is reflected in—and even determined by—our emotional reactions to events, happy and tragic. When good things happen, we believe that God is good. But when sorrowful experiences occur, we can come to believe that God does not love us and will always deal severely with us. When Satan seduced Eve in the Garden, he attacked her theology. In the same way, the shameful, painful events of the adult child's life have the ability to form his view of God through transference, which means projecting beliefs and impressions gained in one relationship onto someone else. In this case, God.

God's discipline does not come from the hand of an abusive parent whose desires are selfish, demonic and punitive. His discipline sets boundaries that produce security. He prunes back growth, closes doors, reproves us and sometimes temporarily disappoints us—for our highest good. Our understanding of God will always be under attack and subject to the erosion that comes from transference, apathy, mistrust, the devil's suggestions, deception and the myriad of emotions you feel from day to day. But the truth is that God doesn't change. Jesus Christ is the same—yesterday and today and forever (Hebrews 13:8).

How do we change our theology? How do we learn to trust the perfect goodness of God? To know that He is *always* working for our good?

By pursuing Him. David said, "I sought the Lord, and He heard me, and delivered me from all my fears" (Psalm 34:4, KJV). The Lord is always good to the soul that seeks Him, and the wounded soul must seek Him if it is ever to be healed. Almost every person who ever received miraculous blessings from Jesus left where he was and went to where God was.

One of the greatest deceptions created by the adult child syndrome is the passive spirit that takes everything life deals lying down. It is as though all of this person's will, hope and desire to try have evaporated. He can no longer believe that somewhere a God is moving who can change things. What delights the heart of God are those who pursue Him with expectancy, who believe. True faith acts. "I will arise and go to my father," said the Prodigal Son as he began his long journey back home.

Receiving emotional healing means taking the words you have heard, beginning to implement them and watching God restore your wounded soul to full health. You can choose to walk the pathway that leads out of the curse and into the blessing of the Lord. You can begin a new legacy now—for your days ahead and for your children and for their children.

Do you wish to get well? Then may the Lord bless you as you move into His healing grace.

Healing Prayer

Dear heavenly Father, almighty God,

Today I choose life for me and my descendants after me. I have observed the dysfunctional, cursed ways of my past and determine not to do likewise, but instead to walk out of their power over me. I determine to break every one with Your all-powerful help. I want You to adopt me as Your child. Take me into Your loving arms and restore my wounded soul. I give You permission to discipline me for my highest good. I want to stay in the limits set only by Your love, reaching out into the wonderful plan You have for me. Help me forgive those who have passed on a curse to me. Let the blessing of the Lord fall upon them from now on. In Jesus' name. Amen.